The Story
of Montgomery

The Story
of Montgomery

by

Ann & John Welton

Logaston Press

LOGASTON PRESS
Little Logaston, Logaston,
Woonton, Almeley, Herefordshire HR3 6QH

First published by Logaston Press 2003
Copyright © Ann & John Welton 2003

ISBN 1 904396 05 4 (hardback)
ISBN 1 904396 09 7 (paperback)

Set in Baskerville & Times by Logaston Press
and printed in Great Britain by
The Cromwell Press, Trowbridge, Wiltshire

*Cover illustration: Print by Hooper showing the view of Montgomery from the
Welshpool road, dated 1786*
*Illustration on previous page: An early photograph of Arthur Street c.1880 showing the
Wynnstay Arms, the wheelwright's shop, the house eventually to accommodate the bank
prior to the addition of the stucco frontage and the Town Hall with the open arches
Rear cover. Top: The Constable's staff, now held in the Old Bell Museum
Middle: Watercolour of the church by John Ingleby, 1793
Bottom: Print of the interior of the church, drawn sometime between 1859 and 1875*

To the people of Montgomery, both past and present

What is the use of a book, thought Alice, without pictures or conversations?

Contents

Acknowledgments

On 13 April 1973 an open meeting held in Montgomery Town Hall resulted in the formation of Montgomery Civic Society. The first Chairman was Dr. J.D.K. Lloyd and the authors were both founder members. One of the first projects the new society undertook was a very successful exhibition of old photographs. This was followed by a series of exhibitions resulting in an increasingly large collection of local photographs and other ephemera. A home was found eventually for these with the establishment by the society of the Old Bell Museum in Arthur Street. The authors' personal collection together with the museum's archive and images from many other different sources has supplied the material for this book.

Early encouragement to produce an illustrated book about the town came from two of our members, Janet and Colin Bord who with their professional knowledge and publishing experience guided us in the management of our rapidly expanding collection of early photographs. It was, however, not until a few years later that members of the Powysland Club, in particular Eric Gent, Glyn Tegai Hughes, Melvyn Humphreys and Daphne Woodhouse, prompted us to make a start and together with the help of Dr. Peter Ashton the project got underway. Peter's contribution in much of the early planning of the book was invaluable and we are particularly grateful to have had access to his Tape Talks to the Blind in which he recorded the memories of old Montgomery residents in the 1970s.

In Montgomery we have been fortunate in having made the acquaintance of a number of eminent historians and archaeologists, many of whom have become close friends. The late Philip Barker and his family and Bob Higham have involved us and many other people in the town in their long-term excavations at Hen Domen. Jeremy Knight has been generous in sharing his knowledge of Montgomery castle following the archaeological excavations.

Many local people have helped and influenced us in the writing of this book. Sadly, Dr. J.D.K. Lloyd did not live long enough to see the establishment of the Old Bell Museum, but his extensive list of published articles and legacy of handwritten notes have been invaluable. We are deeply indebted to Raymond and Sylvia Pidgeon. We have drawn extensively upon Raymond's research into the buildings in the town and the history of the gaols in Montgomery. Sylvia's constructive comments about some of the draft chapters have been most helpful. We have greatly enjoyed many productive discussions and arguments with Arthur Baldwin whose knowledge of the local vernacular architecture is quite remarkable.

In several of the subjects we have covered, certain people and families have made significant contributions. David Evans' assistance regarding Civil War affairs has been much appreciated, as has Ivor Tanner's intimate knowledge of the building of the stone castle. We are grateful to Stephen Hayes for his assistance with the church history and to the James family for the use of their extensive family archive, which has added much personal interest to the chapel section. Meurick Jones, Peter and Elaine English and Morris Marshall & Poole have kindly supplied information and pictures for the chapter on markets. The Bunner family have allowed us to copy some of their family photographs and use data from original research into the history of their business. Members of the Weaver family and past and present members of the Fire Service have been generous in supplying us with information and other material, which we have used in the book. Harry Williams' enthusiastic help, with his lifelong involvement in sport, in particular cricket, has been invaluable.

Others who have willingly helped with advice regarding a large range of subjects are: Dick Banton, Rev. Michael Collis, Tony Constable, Richard Coy, Flossie Evans, Mike Evans, Mansel and Anne Griffiths, Beryl Hale, Mr. & Mrs. M. Hughes, Phil Jennings, the late Noel Jerman, Helen Jones, Sidney Lloyd, Montgomery Town Council Members and past Town Clerks, Nick, Eva and Sally Moore, Lys and Trevor Morris, Trevor Pugh, Nick Randall-Smith, Brinley Robinson, David Thomas, Dr. Geoff Threlfall, Dafydd Vickers, Gregynog Press, Jean Williams, Dr. Sioned Williams, Margaret Worthington, Michael Worthington-Williams and Dr. John Wynn-Jones.

The images in the book have come from many sources and in the following list we would like to express our thanks to the following, with apologies for any omissions: the Bainbridge family, the late Cecily Behrmann, Thelma Bevan, Terry Boundy and family, Eva Bredsdorff, Mrs. Clubb, the late Clara Davies, Norman Davies, Tecwyn and Maureen Davies, the late Les Evans, Lynn Evans, Mike Evans, Dorothy Gamble, Verdun Gornall, Fr. Anthony and Ann Hirst, Dr. Chris Humphreys, Philip Humphreys, the late R.W.P. (Walter) Humphreys, Marjorie Jones and the Bayliss family, Gerald Joseph, Betty Kinsey, Barbara Legge, Bryony Mansfield, Mrs. McCleary, Sue and Mark Michaels, Bill and Sally Orme, Philip Panton, the late Edith and Jack Powell, Phyllis Price, the late David Proctor, the late C. S. Pryce, Mrs. M.E. Price, the Earl of Powis, the late Mary Read, Marjory and Brian Richards, Peter Scholefield, John Sewell, Margaret Stacey, Arthur Tanner and family, Tom Till, Chris Tomley, the late Jo Tomley, Joyce Venables, Tom and Dolly Weaver, the late Alice Williams, C.B. Williams, Helen Williams.

Particular mention must be made here of Chris Welton's meticulous work in the preparation of the images for publication. The quality of many of the pictures is a reflection of his skill and patience.

We are grateful to the following organisations for the help we have received in the preparation of the book: CADW, Clwyd-Powys Archaeological Trust, National Library of Wales, National Museum of Wales, Newtown Library (local studies), Powys County Archives, Powysland Club Library, Powysland Museum, Royal Armouries Leeds, Royal Commission for Ancient and Historic Monuments in Wales, Shropshire Records and Research Centre.

We have enjoyed working with Andy Johnson of Logaston Press and have very much appreciated his deadlines. We are grateful for his support, advice and encouragement in the publication of this book.

Preface

The writing of this book has long been in the minds of the authors. There can be few communities with such a small population as the old county town of Montgomery, which can boast such a rich and fascinating heritage. The daunting task of collating the extensive collection of illustrative material together with the long and already well-documented history into a cohesive, interesting and attractive volume has been a real challenge.

We have chosen as chapter headings subjects that we feel will be of interest to all who read them and perhaps, with some self indulgence, those about which we have most enjoyed learning. It has not been our intention to produce a comprehensive, detailed or learned historical discourse about Montgomery, but rather to give all our readers an accurate, but easily assimilated illustrated story of times past. We have tried to make each chapter come alive through the stories of real people, many who lived long ago and might well become forgotten, but all of whom have helped to shape the way the town has developed.

Having lived and worked in the town of Montgomery for over half our lifetimes, we have been privileged to meet and get to know many of the older members of the community some of whose families can boast many generations of residence here. It is from them that much of the information in this book comes, but the final responsibility for all the details in the text must rest on our shoulders and we sincerely apologise for any inaccuracies or omissions.

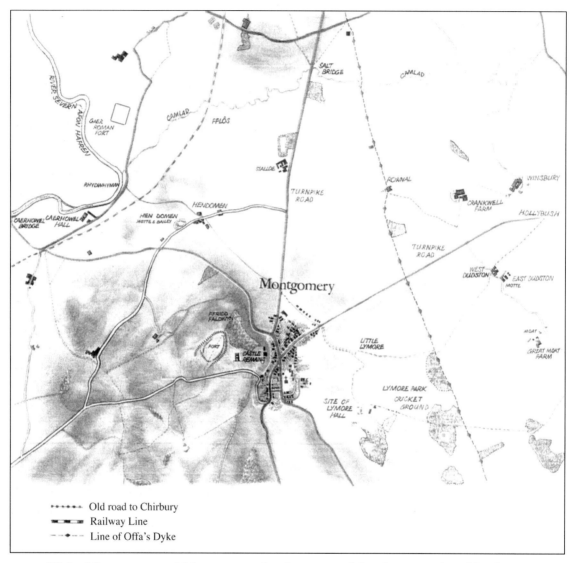

Map of the area around Montgomery, showing many of the places mentioned in the text

1 Introduction

Starting as a trickle from a spring on the slopes of Plynlimon the River Severn gains strength as it winds eastwards through Mid Wales towards England. Close to the border its flow is supplemented by two important tributaries, the River Camlad from the east and the River Rhiew from the west. The lowest point of the river that can regularly be forded is a little way upstream from the mouth of the Camlad some two miles north-west of Montgomery and is known as Rhydwhyman.

This historic ford was at one time the traditional meeting place between the Welsh and English and has always been regarded as of great strategic importance. Countless men and horses must have used this crossing through the millennia, picking their way over the stones and boulders, pleased to gain access to the bank at the other side. It was this ford that determined much of the subsequent development of the communities in the area of Montgomery.

As far back as Neolithic times the ford was guarded by a fort, which was later greatly extended by Iron Age man. This huge camp with its massive earthworks stands high on a hill overlooking the ford and is now known as Ffridd Faldwyn.[1] In the first century AD the Romans built a large camp, Forden Gaer (*Lavobrinta*) close to the River Severn downstream from the ford. In its day it was a busy staging post connected with a network of roads to and from other Roman sites including Wroxeter (*Viroconium*) and the important military post at Caersws (*Mediolanum*). It remained in use for over 300 years, serving the dual purpose of defending the area and controlling the ancient river crossing.

The extraordinary and impressive Dyke, probably built on the orders of King Offa of Mercia, runs for a mile or so, close to Montgomery, where it still defines the national, county and parish boundary. Built towards the end of the 8th century, there have been different theories as to why and how it was constructed. The most plausible explanation would seem to be that it was intended as a defensible structure, and that it was built by local labour under overall supervision. Whatever the explanation, it has measured the border for over 1,200 years.

The defeat of King Harold's army on 14 October 1066, in the fiercely fought battle of Hastings, led to the imposition of Norman rule over the land. Wales was invaded in 1068 and in order to keep his land, King William granted large estates to his nobles and barons. Prominent among these was Roger de Montgomery, related to the King, who had been entrusted not only with the defence of Normandy during William's absence, but also with the safety of William's wife, the Duchess Mathilda, and the rest of her family. He was

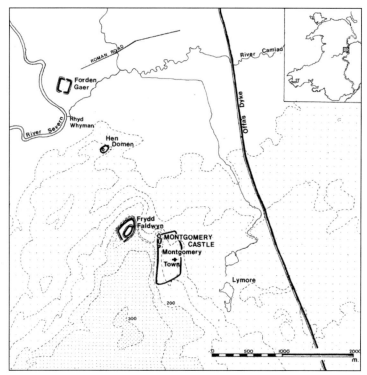

*Map showing the major historic sites
around the town of Montgomery*

*Part of the Bayeaux tapestry
showing a motte and bailey
castle under construction*

*Reconstruction drawing of excavated areas in the bailey
of the Norman motte and bailey castle of Hen Domen
by Peter Scholefield*

rewarded for his loyalty with gifts of lands in Sussex around Arundel and Chichester and in 1071 received a large area of the Welsh Marches and was created Earl of Shrewsbury. The strategic importance of the ford at Rhydwhyman would soon have been pointed out to Roger and work on his new earth and timber castle,[2] now called Hen Domen, about a mile from the present town, was quickly under way. The site he chose had at one time been a ploughed field and later abandoned as part of a hunting chase. That Earl Roger of Montgomery chose to call it after his native home in Normandy is an indication of the importance he placed on the castle. It is the source of the name passed on to the present town, which subsequently gave its title to the county of which it was the shire town, covering a huge part of central Wales. It could have been his original aim to build a

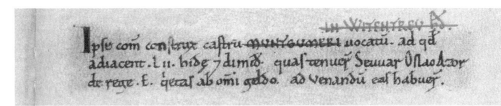

Reference to Montgomery in the Domesday Book 1085

town and a priory by his new castle, for this was a common practice of the Norman lords of that time. It is possible that, beneath the small hamlet of Hendomen, there may well lie the foundations of an earlier settlement which would naturally have grown up around the motte and bailey castle.

In 1085 King William told his council that he wanted a record of every part of his kingdom and the following year his agents travelled throughout England. Their findings were recorded and preserved in two huge volumes at Winchester and were known as the Domesday Book. Here is found the first written reference to Montgomery which at that time, as an English castle, was included in Shropshire:

'Ipse comes construxit castrum muntgumery vocatum'

The earl himself has built a castle called MONTGOMERY to
which belong $52^{1}/_{2}$ hides which Siward, Oslac [and] Azur held
of King Edward quit of all geld. They had these for the chase ...
These lands three thegns held. Now Earl Roger hold them.
They are and were waste.

In 1094 Roger was succeeded by his second son, Hugh. When Hugh was killed in 1098 his elder brother, Robert de Bellême took over the tenure. Robert's revolt against Henry I in 1102 resulted in his removal from England. He was eventually captured in Normandy in 1112 and imprisoned in Corfe Castle until his death in 1130. After the fall of the Montgomery family, the king passed the castle to Baldwin de Boulers and it is from their family that the Welsh name of Trefaldwyn arises—*Tre-Faldwyn* means Baldwin's Town. Following Baldwin de Boulers, Hen Domen passed to William Courteney, thence to the king and finally to Gwenwynwyn, Prince of Powys, after which the new stone castle was begun.

In the autumn of 1223, one hundred and fifty years after Roger had built his motte and bailey castle at Hendomen, the royal army, having relieved the de Breos castle of Builth from siege by Llewelyn ap Iorwerth, travelled north to Montgomery through Hereford, Leominster and Shrewsbury. The young King Henry III was accompanied by his justiciar, Hubert de Burgh and other military advisers and was shown the great rocky outcrop on which it was proposed to build an impregnable stone castle. The date was 1 October 1223, his sixteenth birthday.

Anxiety had been growing concerning the security of the Marches since Llewelyn was allied with the French and with the baronial opposition, although some Welsh leaders had seen the truce between Louis of France and the English in September 1217 as a betrayal by Louis of his allies. It had become increasingly evident that given its political and military position, which could no longer be adequately guarded by an obsolete castle of earth and timber, priority should be given to the positioning of a substantial garrison at Montgomery at the most strategically important point of the region.

The proposed new fortress was to be a massive structure. When complete, the castle, the outer walls of which were lime-washed white, would have presented a most impressive appearance. It provided a formidable stronghold for the English kings until the end of the thirteenth century, when Edward I built his great castles scattered around the coastal areas of Wales and at Builth, thus diminishing Montgomery's military importance.

The stormy years of conflict between the English and the Welsh in the first seventy years of the castle's existence are described in great detail by Paul Remfry.[3] The subsequent history of the castle included periods of neglect and rebuilding until the Civil War. By 1622 the living conditions in the old castle had become so uncomfortable that a brick

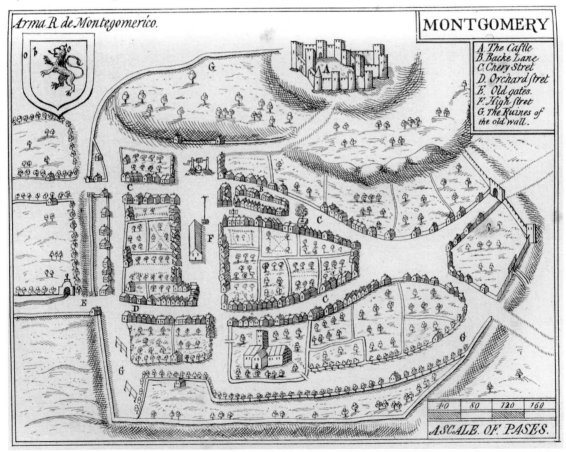

Plan of Montgomery Town from John Speed's county map of Montgomeryshire, 1610. This includes the only surviving drawing of Montgomery Castle and although rather simplistic it would appear to correspond accurately with contemporary descriptions. One can also see the medieval street layout, the town walls with the four gates and the original guildhall or market hall in the centre of the main street

mansion, described later as having been 'an elegant and noble pile', was built in the shelter of the walls of the middle ward. Both house and castle were soon to be embroiled in the Civil War. David Evans, of Princes Street, who has had a lifelong interest in this period, has kindly contributed the following account of the Battle of Montgomery:

Print by Hooper showing the view of Montgomery from the Welshpool road, dated 1786

Edward, Lord Herbert of Chirbury who was living in the mansion in the middle ward of the castle in 1644 was caught up in the full fury of the Civil War when, in September of that year, Parliamentary forces having captured a vital gunpowder convoy at nearby Newtown turned their attention to Montgomery Castle, believing, correctly, that it was poorly defended. On their approach, the town militia melted away and Lord Herbert's servants either fled or begged him not to resist, compelling him to make terms and surrender the fortress without a shot being fired, an action that triggered the Battle of Montgomery, which took place on 18 September to the north of the town.

The surrender brought about a swift counter attack from all available Royalist forces in Shropshire, who caught the outnumbered Parliamentarians in open ground, foraging for supplies. The cavalry, under Sir Thomas Myddleton of Chirk withdrew towards Oswestry, leaving the infantry to seek refuge within the castle walls. A full-scale siege began immediately. Within a fortnight two more opposing armies arrived in the area; a Royalist column from Chester and north Wales under John, Lord Byron, while Myddleton returned with a combined force under Sir John Meldrum, Sir William Brereton and Sir William Fairfax. Key aspects of the major pitched battle which occurred on 18 September, the largest in Wales during the First Civil War of 1642-46, remain obscure, as the events are poorly documented. What is clear is that the larger Royalist army was crushingly defeated, leaving some 500 dead, 1,500 prisoners and all their desperately needed arms and supplies lost. The Royalist defeat was decisive for the conduct of the entire war. All hope of using the north Wales and Marcher forces to attempt a re-conquest of the northern counties of England, lost after Marston Moor, was gone, and the surviving Royalists, henceforth, were compelled to fight a purely defensive war from increasingly beleaguered garrisons.

Montgomery was garrisoned for Parliament until Lord Herbert's death in August 1648, when it passed to his son Richard, an ardent Royalist. The fate of the castle was effectively sealed and the order was made to render it indefensible and it was demolished in 1649.

In the years after the King's visit in 1223, the planned new town of Montgomery was laid out below the new castle. In 1227 a royal charter was granted which allowed the new burgesses to enclose the town with a ditch and a wall and gave them the right to hold fairs at the feasts of St. Bartholomew and All Saints and a weekly market on Thursdays.

A North View of the Town and Castle of MONTGOMERY, in North-Wales. July 9th 1784.

Montgomery, a clean little Town romantically situated at the foot of craggy hills at the head of a pleasant plain through which the Severn glides in beautiful Meanders, sends Members to Parliament; it buildings are but indifferent its greatest Ornament is its Town hall lately built probably at the Expence of the Earl of Powis as the Arms of that Family are over its principal front.

The Castle & Town were built by Valdioin or Baldwin, Lieutenant of the Marches of Wales, in the reign of Will.m the Conqueror, for which reason the Britons call it Trewaldwyn or Baldwin's Town; but the English are said to have named it Montgomery, from Roger Montgomery, to whom William had given the Earldoms of Arundel & Shrewsbury, who gained the Castle & town of Baldwin. The Castle was afterwards demolished by the Welch, but William Rufus reedified it in 1093, and it was burnt by King Henry the 3d. in 1232. But being afterwards rebuilt it became the Seat of the Lords Herbert of Cherbury. It was since ruined in the Civil Wars of King Charles the 1st. since which time it has been neglected & is now a mere heap of ruins. the unshapen appearance of the Walls did not seem as if they would recompence the trouble of climbing up for a closer inspection. I therefore contented myself in taking the above Sketch from a Station about a quarter of a mile from the Town on the road to Welch-pool.

Edward Herbert, first Baron of Cherbury & Author of a book entitled the History of the Life & Reign of King Henry the 8th. was born in this Castle in 1581 he died Augt 20th 1648 & was buried in the Church of St. Giles's in the Fields, London.

Page from Topographical Collections, Monmouthshire and Wales *by Rev. John Pridden, 1784, published by kind permission of the National Library of Wales*

In the first few months of the stone castle's construction a chapel was added and by 1227 there is reference to the church in 'New' Montgomery town. When new towns were laid out in the traditional grid pattern an area was always reserved for the church, and the crest of the small hill that comprises the east side of the town was the chosen site.

After the Civil War Montgomery gradually prospered and developed into a busy market town. In the eighteenth and early nineteenth centuries many of the houses were given Georgian frontages and the new Town Hall replaced the old Market Hall, which stood in the middle of the main street. By then the Assize courts were being held in the Town Hall and Montgomery had become the county town of Montgomeryshire. From the time of the first charter the town was governed by two bailiffs and the hereditary burgesses, but new changes took place in 1885 when the government was invested in an elected mayor and corporation. Further changes in local government in 1974 resulted in the town losing its borough status but retaining its town council.

Because of its geographical site on the side of the hill beneath the castle rock, Montgomery was firstly bypassed by the canal and later by the railway. Neighbouring towns developed whilst the old county town, virtually unchanged, remains one of the finest examples of an unspoilt medieval new town.

Montgomery has featured in many itineraries of the tours of the Principality by the early gentlemen travellers and their often quaintly written journals with their frequent inaccuracies record their differing impressions of the town and make fascinating reading:

1754 Dr. Richard Pococke
'there is a handsome new market place in the town. It [the town] is a small poor place and chiefly subsists by its markets'.[4]

1770 Pennant
'Montgomery, a small neat town, partly built on the slope, partly on the summit of a hill beneath the shadow of a much higher'.[5]

1771 Nathaniel Spencer Esq.
'the town is at present a very polite place, there being many families of distinction constantly residing in it and there are several good streets with very fine houses'.[6]

1774 Lord George Lyttleton
'Montgomery town is no better than a village'.[7]

1784 John Byng
'Montgomery is a small town, romantically situated, consisting of little more than a town hall, and a gaol (oddly call'd the College,) the church yard commands a view (over the bowling green) of a fine valley: Limner Park [Lymore Park, for which see later] &c.: and several new made graves ornamented with flowers: ... One gravestone bears the extraordinary Xtian name of Whatsoever Warmort. After our tea, passing by the college, we survey'd the ruins of the old castle, of which but little remains'.[8]

1798 Rev. J. Evans

'Having ideally supposed that the County Town must be superior to all others from the point of beauty and extent; we were disappointed to find it a small place consisting of about one hundred half timbered houses forming a miserable street ... In the upper part of it stands the Guildhall, a handsome stone building where the sessions are held in rotation with [Welsh]Poole ... At the bottom stood a large mansion, called Black-Hall the seat of the Herberts, long since destroyed by fire: and a deep foss now marks the scite where once it stood'.[9]

2   Town and Castle

The northern parish boundary of Montgomery follows the winding River Camlad before it crosses the road from Welshpool at the Salt Bridge, the name of which is possibly a corruption of the Welsh *Is allt* meaning below the ascent or steep hill. It is from this direction that many visitors gain their first sight of the unmistakable and unforgettable skyline of the town. It nestles comfortably in the shallow sloping valley defined on one side by the massive ruins of the castle on its rocky outcrop and the parish church on the other.

Up until about forty years ago, the castle's crumbling masonry overlooking the town was generally regarded just as a romantic ruin. It was the place to visit to enjoy wonderful views along the Severn valley to Welshpool and along the Camlad and Rea valleys towards Shrewsbury, to picnic and no doubt to go courting. Little thought was given to what lay under the plateau of grass covered mounds and depressions together with the few massive chunks of unidentified masonry. Although it is known that drawings and plans of the castle

Eighteenth-century print showing the town nestling between the castle ruins on the right and the church on the left

9

Drawing of the castle ruins in 1742 by Samuel and Nathaniel Buck

were ordered to be made before the large scale demolition carried out in 1649, none of these have ever been found. John Speed's map of 1610 contains the only known pre-demolition drawing but its scale is so small that it is only of limited value. Samuel and Nathaniel Bucks' somewhat romantic drawing of 1742 shows considerably more masonry than exists today. A major collapse around 1800 resulted in the appearance much as it was prior to the excavations.

In 1963 the owner, Lord Powis, placed the castle in the guardianship of the Ministry of Public Buildings and Works, later to become CADW. Conservation work and excava-

The castle ruins in 1925 many years before the conservation and excavation work started

The new walk to the castle from the conduit, through the trees, shortly after it had been made c.1900

tions commenced the following year and gradually the true extent of the fortress was revealed.[1] The site on which the castle was built is described in the extract from the survey of 1593 (see p.121) as on a ridge running north and south. It is protected by steep cliffs to the north and east with a valley to the west. The approach from the south, however, is along level ground and the defences here were designed to present a successive series of obstacles to possible attack. The first of these, utilising a natural feature, was an outer barbican a few yards to the north of the Old Castle Farm. Next were the outer and inner ditches, which extend the full width of the ridge. A few days after the visit of Henry III twenty miners were sent without delay from the Forest of Dean to excavate these. They also had the task of flattening the top of the north end of the ridge to enable the massive defensive twin-towered inner gatehouse and the walls of the inner ward to be built. In addition,

Two young men from the Powell family of Chapel Place enjoy a smoke below the well tower

The castle ruins and time to sit and read and chat

a large area around the castle rock was ordered to be cleared of woodland. To ensure the speedy erection of a defensible structure, much of the early building work was carried out by carpenters using massive timbers, work subsequently replaced with stone by masons. Miners were also employed in sinking the remarkable well adjacent to the inner ward through over 200 feet of solid rock. The D-shaped well tower was added later. Between 1251 and 1253 the middle ward was enclosed with curtain walls together with a twin-towered gatehouse overlooking the outer ditch.

The excavations commenced in 1964 revealed just how extensive the castle was and enabled more to be learnt about life there in medieval times. Originally, the ground floor of the inner ward gatehouse had a guardroom on one side, a prison on the other and on the floor above was a chapel and the 'Knights chamber'. In the later medieval period, the inner ward contained a kitchen with a large bake-oven and a brewhouse and in the sixteenth and seventeenth centuries the curtain walls were lined with lodgings and stables. The well was found to be filled with demolition debris to the depth of 54m. (177ft.) and it was only when this was cleared in 1974 that some really noteworthy items were discovered. Ivor Tanner, who was foreman of the labour force at the time and personally responsible for removing many tons of masonry, says that the most exciting day of his life was when he discovered the completely intact, iron bound, wooden well-bucket at a depth of 55.2m. Many other artefacts, including a pewter candlestick, a leather pistol holder, over fifty wooden vessels and many animal bones, were recovered. At 62.4m the excavation of the well was terminated mainly on safety grounds.

The final entry in the survey of 1593[2] gives an indication of the dilapidated state of the castle at that time: 'There ys noe howsholde stuffe in the Castell but onlie a brassen boyling potte, ijo sesterns of leadd and one lytle peece of waynscotte remayninge in the grett hall or dyning Chamber'. At that time Sir Edward Herbert was living at his new house, Black Hall. In 1622 his grandson, also Sir Edward Herbert (to be created Lord Herbert of Chirbury) engaged a family of builders from Hertfordshire by the name of Scampion to build a new house[3] for him in the middle ward which had until then contained lodgings and stables. This was built of brick and completely transformed the middle ward. It was remembered as 'an elegant and noble pile, beautiful without and richly furnished within, the Lord Herbert having expended many thousand pounds therein, and his library was an ornament thereto and abundantly replenisht with Books of his own purchasing and choyce'. It was outside

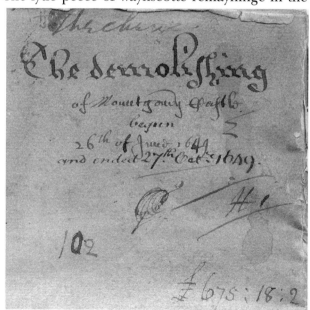

1649 document stating the price of the demolition of Montgomery Castle

the main entrance of this house, on the site of the old middle ward gate-house that Sir Thomas Myddleton, on 4 September 1644 threatened to explode a petard if Lord Edward Herbert did not surrender his castle. He did and despite the ensuing battle the fate of the castle was sealed. The castle was virtually razed to the ground by miners, masons and a large force of labourers using explosives between 26 June and 27 October 1649 at a cost of £675. 18s. 2d.

To understand the visual impact that the castle would have had on the thirteenth- and fourteenth-century visitor one needs to use considerable imagination. Selecting the tallest piece of existing masonry and multiplying its height by two will give a rough idea of the original height of the curtain walls; the towers were considerably higher. It would have been a truly formidable fortress in its early days.

The approach to the town from the north must have been regarded as the most important, as here can be found the only stretch of the town walls made of stone. Elsewhere they were constructed of earth, probably surmounted with a wooden palisade. The four gates—Ceri, Cedewain, Chirbury and Arthur—gained their names from the ancient neighbouring lordships to which they led, Arthur being a sixteenth century corruption of Gortheur.

Two of the main routes out of the town have changed over the centuries. The old road to Chirbury followed a winding route via Burnt House and the Dudston farms, rejoining the existing road near the Hollybush Cottages. The present dead straight road, which cuts through Offa's Dyke, is often mistakenly thought to be Roman. It was made as a result of

The turnpike road to Chirbury showing the old tollgate standing at the junction with New Road and the Lymore Lane, on the fringe of the town, c.1920

13

the Turnpike act in the second half of the seventeenth century, and in order to prevent evasion of the payment of tolls, it was enacted that

> it should be lawful for the trustees to stop up and discontinue the lane or way leading from the Hollybush Cottage in Winsbury through Dudson [Dudston] to Montgomery; from the Hollybush Cottage, through Winsbury to Round Hill [Rownal]; from the said Hollybush to the Timberth Lane ...[4]

The old timber-framed tollgate cottage, which stood at the crossroads where New Road meets Chirbury Road, was dismantled in 1969. It was reassembled as an extension to Crogbren; originally a small 'hall house' in an area referred to in old documents as Top of Town. The only tollgates still remaining are at Sarkley, Stalloe and at the Pen-y-bryn turn, just beyond Llwynobin, on the road to Bishop's Castle.

The old route to Newtown originally left the Welshpool road just beyond the Verlon farm, past Sarkley and the Clift Cottage (now Woodpecker Hall), rejoining the present road at the crossroads near Hendomen House. The road below the castle rock ended at the small group of cottages that included the Piggin Tavern, opposite the quarry where stone for the New Gaol was obtained. It was extended in the middle of the 1840s and became known as the Station Road. Originally, about quarter of a mile along, just beyond where the post-war house named Jamesford View now stands, the new road took a very sharp curve to the left and then to the right over a small stream. This dangerous feature, which can still be clearly seen, became known as Penson's Twist after Thomas Penson the County Surveyor of the time. Later a culvert was made for the stream and the curve eliminated.

For the first three or four hundred years of

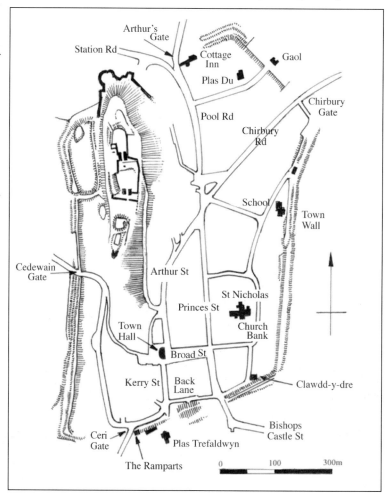

Plan of the town

14

Montgomery's existence nearly all the houses would have made of timber, wattle and daub and thatched with straw, all of which were in plentiful local supply. Following the demolition of the castle in 1649, a variety of secondhand materials became available. Many of the walls within the town and the stonework in some of the older houses include stone robbed from the castle ruins sometimes including pieces of red sandstone that quite possibly had earlier been taken from the priory in Chirbury. Around the same time, bricks began to appear, some undoubtedly from Edward Herbert's mansion in the middle ward of the castle, but others newly made in the vicinity. Quite a few of the bigger farms had their own

A modern bungalow, Ceri Bryn, now stands on the site of this old cottage photographed c.1910

kilns for making bricks, the remains of the one at Stalloe can still be found. Two of the tenants of Stalloe brickyard who stamped their bricks with their names were Maurice Jones and Arthur Vaughan.

In addition to Lymore Hall, which has deserved a chapter to itself, there were numerous other old buildings within the town which have long since gone or been altered beyond recognition. Some leave only a memory but happily some also a photographic record, as in the case of the long, low, thatched cottage which once stood in Pool Road, probably the last of its type in the town. Of the cluster of small cottages which once stood near the site of Ceri Gate and the house called the Ramparts, some are likewise recorded. Photographs of the town taken from the castle in the early 1920s show a number of buildings which have disappeared. The timber-framed cottage seen next to the Presbyterian Chapel was demolished when the Manse was built, whilst the large brewery and malt house behind the Buck Hotel, for a time the

An old thatched cottage in Pool Road opposite Manor House was possibly the last of its type in Montgomery. It has been replaced by a brick-built terrace of three houses

Ceri Gate Cottages c.1910

15

Two views of Myrtle Cottage and Bank Cottage on the corner of Kerry Road
and the road to Llandyssil between 1910 and 1930

home of the Calvinistic Methodists, are no longer there. The adjacent Buck Yard used to contain a terrace of three cramped dwellings known as Thornloe Cottages. In Kerry Street, nearly all of the houses on the west side were taken down in three stages between 1938 and

Princes Street showing the Presbyterian Chapel with the black and white cottage to its right and Bevan's yard to its left. Spout House in the foreground with its stables, at one time housed the groom to the doctor from the White House next door in Arthur Street. Centre right, the extensive brewery and malthouse buildings together with Thornloe Cottages can be seen to the rear of the Buck Hotel

Kerry Street houses just prior to their demolition in the 1960s. The shop at the far end was Williams bakery

Kerry Street with its cobbled pavements in the 1880s. The Gullet Inn can be seen at the end of the black and white terrace of houses

1966, starting with the old Gullet Inn, all to be replaced by council accommodation. The 1960s saw many changes in Montgomery. The Crown Cottages in Back Lane and the Thornloe Cottages were demolished at much the same time. The tan yard buildings together with the extremely old, timber-framed Well House were cleared by the council

Kerry Street houses being demolished. The closeness of the timbers of these houses indicate that they may have been amongst the oldest in the town

Arthur Street. Beyond the black and white houses a group of houses opposite Bunner's shop can be seen. One of these was the home of Mr. McGavin the veterinary surgeon

to make available land to build the old peoples' bungalows in what was appropriately named Well Street. The three houses which stood on the site of the small garden opposite Bunner's, one originally a shop and another the home of Mr. McGavin, a veterinary surgeon at the turn of the century, were also to go. The 1970s saw the old stone building known as Poston's Farm in Chirbury Road disappear to make room for the Chirbury Gate council estate and in the 1980s the crumbling old terrace of houses built above the Pound by Samuel Rowe, about two hundred years before, was sympathetically replaced, retaining its original name of Rowes Terrace.

The newly built Tan-y-Graig Terrace, prior to occupation in 1937—the first houses to be built by the council in Montgomery

The first purpose-built council accommodation in Montgomery was the terrace of four houses called Tan-y-Graig in Pool Road, erected between the wars. The Tan-y-mur estate was first developed in the 1950s and later extended in stages to finally include Lymore View. The old peoples' bungalows in Kerry Gate were among the last council developments.

18

Bishop's Castle Street in 1910. The extensive allotment area
was to be the future site of the Tan-y-mur housing estate

The years around 1900 saw a number of fairly large houses being built for some of the better off residents. Tre Llydiart was built in Chirbury Road in 1900 for the solicitor C.S. Pryce, by the firm of Hughes from Marton who were also responsible for the Baptist Chapel. Plas Du in Gaol Road was built in 1901 for the Vaughan family by Maurice Jones, Brynawel opposite the school for Charles James and at about the same time Ael-y-Bryn for Mr. Henry Jones of Sutton. Over recent years there has been a steady increase in the building of private housing.

Plas Du under construction in 1900.
After enlargement, the imprint A VAUGHAN STALLOE
can be made out on the heap of bricks
in front of the wheelbarrow

The newly built Institute in 1924

*Old half-timbered wheelwright's house
in Arthur Street, which was
demolished in the 1920s
to provide a site for the Institute*

The Institute was a very handsome gift to the townspeople of Montgomery from David Davies of Broneirion, Llandinam, and Member of Parliament for Montgomeryshire. It was one of a number of Institutes he donated to communities within the county. Built on a site in Arthur Street given by Alderman Nicholas Fairles Humphreys, that once contained an old thatched timber-framed wheelwright's shop, it was designed and purpose-built by Messrs. Ridge and Haynes of Oswestry and cost upwards of £4,000.

The original plans showed that there were public baths with hot and cold water, a library and newsroom with fitted newspaper racks and shelving, committee room, refreshment room, lock up shop, billiard room, bar for the sale of non intoxicating drinks, and had quarters for a caretaker. It was designed with a central heating installation and was even wired up for electricity in anticipation of its eventual availability in the town. The gift also included all the furnishings, china, a billiard table and a piano.

When David Davies and his wife handed over the building to the town on 19 February 1924 he said 'if you will make use of it abundantly it will be the greatest gratitude you can show to us for whatever we have done towards its establishment'. His philosophy was that the institute should be used for recreation in the broadest sense, 'not merely for the playing of games and amusement, but also for the improvement of the mind through intellectual pursuits'.[5] The building is still owned by the town council and run for the benefit of the community.

Clawdd-y-dre, as its name implies, lies on the Town Ditch and is now quite a substantial residence. The original building was probably a small and modest timber-framed cottage to which successive generations have added extra wings and storeys. Henry Whittingham, a bailiff in George I's reign, recorded his addition in 1726 with his initials and date above the new front door. The Flemish gable on another wing is an unusual feature, other local examples of which can be seen on the Old Castle Farm and the Cock

The view of Clawdd-y-dre from its tennis court c.1920

The Old Castle Farm with its flemish gable

Hotel, Forden. The changes to the house continue with the addition quite recently of a further wing once again featuring a Flemish gable.

The White House in Arthur Street has also been subjected to enlargement over the centuries. In 1977 when the timber framework was fully exposed during extensive repair work, the opportunity was taken to make a careful study of its structure.[6] It was deduced that there were three main stages in the life of the house. It started as a simple rectangular dwelling with a single, central, wide 'dormer', built around 1600. Later the dormer was moved to one end and another added. The third stage involved lifting the two dormers to their present height and adding another small one between. There were further extensions much later to the rear of the building. Following exposure, the right hand dormer was found to have the following inscription carved on the tie beam: HUGH BENNET : & JOHAN BENNET : ANNO : 1637. Hugh Bennett was a bailiff in the seventeenth century.

The Lions is one of the largest and most impressive houses in the town and first impressions suggest that it may have

The White House, dating back to the sixteenth century, was for over two hundred years the home of medical practitioners

*The Lions with Rev. F.W. Parker and his family in 18??.
He was the first incumbent to occupy the house
which was rented from Lord Powis*

been built all at one time. An early tithe map, however, shows a wing at the back which no longer exists, and in common with nearly every other building it has been altered during its life. There is a plaque on the side bearing the date 1775, but the house almost certainly predates this. Admiral Sir C.T. Jones who died in 1853 lived there at one time. It first became the rectory when the Rev. F.W. Parker was appointed in 1873 and a succession of incumbents rented it from Lord Powis until the Disestablishment in 1920 when it was acquired by the Church in Wales as the official residence of the parish priest. It was sold in the 1980s and the adjacent modern rectory was built. At least two other buildings, which still exist, have served as rectories in the past. Plas Trefaldwyn was the home of the Rev. M.E. Lloyd, rector for thirty-six years from 1794 who was followed by his nephew Rev. Maurice Lloyd until 1873. Although no written records have been found to confirm it, there is little doubt that Glebe House was the earliest existing building to serve as a rectory. It was built on glebe land and an early tithe map shows a footpath leading from the church to its front door.

As mentioned in a later chapter, young Dr. Nicholas Fairles married Miss Mercedes Humphreys in 1877 and moved to live in Bank House. This large house with its beautifully designed conservatory of c.1745 and extensive garden overlooking the town, had been in hands of the Humphreys family for many generations. Following Nicholas Fairles Humphrey's death aged 80 in 1917 the house was rented out. Older residents of the town can remember two heavily laden taxis arriving in Montgomery in 1941 and their unusual passengers, rather reluctantly, stepping out into Broad Street. The group, fearing the bombs or invasion, was 'escaping' from their artistic commune in the Home Counties to the safety of the Welsh hills, hoping to settle in Llanfair Caereinion. Their drivers, once over Offa's Dyke and at a time when petrol was strictly rationed, had refused to take them any further. There were six people in all and they stayed in the Dragon for the night. Within a day or so they had found that Bank House was available and promptly took up its rental. The new tenants comprised the matriarchal Mrs. Mary Agnes Detmold and her son Edward, whose twin brother Maurice had committed suicide about thirty years previously.

The twins were talented and precocious artists and working together had provided illustrations for, among many other books, *Aesop's Fables* and *The Jungle Book*. The others were Edward's sister, Nora, and her husband, Bertram Joy, who was an inventor, Lawrence Biddle whose still life flower paintings were sold to help pay the bills and Harold Hulls, a professor of music and quite an accomplished watercolourist. He soon became very friendly with Miss Florrie Proctor, the local piano teacher. The

Bank House, the home of Dr. Nicholas Watson Fairles Humphreys, with its extensive ornate conservatories and well kept gardens, c.1910

commune's arrival in the town during the war caused quite a stir and much gossip, particularly in view of some of the foreign sounding surnames, which led to the rumour that they might be German spies. One after another they succumbed to illness and died, Edward, however, like his brother, took his own life with a shotgun in 1957, the bloodstains remaining on the stairwell for almost twenty-five years. Nora Joy was the last to go, living on in one rather squalid room as a recluse well into her late nineties. It was only after her death, when over 1,500 paintings were discovered, eventually to be sold at Christies, that the hidden talent of the commune became apparent. During their tenure, the house deteriorated considerably, the roof leaked, causing much damage and the conservatory collapsed beyond repair. The house was eventually sold and apart from the conservatory has been completely restored.

The town of Montgomery has always fascinated the visitor, for its architecture, its ambience, the surrounding scenery and above all for its great sense of history. There can be few places with so many sites of such important historic interest within walking distance of the centre. The account of an early tourist, the Rev. W. Bingley, applies as aptly today as when it was written over two hundred years ago.

In the summer of the year 1798, I was first induced, from the various accounts that had reached me respecting the grandeur of the mountain scenery of North Wales, to appropriate three months to a ramble through all its most interesting parts. [Travelling from Newtown via Llandyssil] the descent continues still beautiful; and, near the town of Montgomery, the fine ruins of its castle formed a very interesting addition to the prospect ... The road is so much elevated immediately above the town, as to afford the traveller a bird's eye view into almost every street.

From the neatness of its houses, [the town] seemed to me to be inhabited principally by persons of small fortune, who had settled here to lead a life of retirement. It is clean, and well built; and seems capable of affording the comforts and conveniences, without any of the bustle and noise of a large town. All the adjacent country is decorated with the most lively and luxuriant scenery.[7]

The view over Montgomery from the Llandyssil road in 2003.
Little has changed since the Rev. Bingley made his observations over two hundred years ago

3   Church and Chapel

The Parish Church of St. Nicholas was founded in the first half of the thirteenth century to serve the new town of Montgomery. Building began soon after work was started on the castle on the raised ground to the south-east of the castle. The size and style of the building soon came to reflect Montgomery's importance.

    The church as it exists today is the result of a constant process of evolution over many centuries.[1] The first building was a simple rectangular stone structure corresponding to the present nave. By the end of the thirteenth century, the north and south transepts had been added and the main body of the church extended to the east by the addition of the

Watercolour of the church and castle in 1793 by John Ingleby. This shows the original porch with its schoolroom and vestry above. Reproduced by kind permission of the National Library of Wales

Detail of Richard Herbert from the tomb in the Lymore Transept

Detail of Magdelan Herbert from the tomb in the Lymore Transept

The Herbert Tomb. The South or Lymore transept was regarded as the responsibility (before disestablishment) of the Herbert family as Lords of the Manor and is dominated by the Elizabethan tomb of Richard Herbert. He was the father of a family which included two famous sons, Edward, 1st Lord Herbert of Chirbury and George Herbert, the divine poet. Under the canopy lie the effigies of Richard and Magdalen Herbert, he dressed in armour and she in a beautifully embroidered dress, behind them are the kneeling figures of their eight children

chancel. The north transept is said to have been built by the Prior of Chirbury (the mother church of Montgomery) for the tenants of Court Calmore, a large wealthy farmstead close to Montgomery. The south transept would in time house the magnificent Elizabethan canopied tomb of Richard Herbert of Montgomery Castle and become known as the Lymore transept after the family's later house near the town. At some time in the sixteenth century, during the time of the dissolution of the monasteries, the ornate rood screen, misericords and stall-work were transferred from Chirbury Priory to be erected in their present positions.

It is appropriate to make reference here to two notable men, both of whom came from families with close connections with the church.

George Herbert the Divine, was the fifth son of Richard Herbert and younger brother of the celebrated Edward Lord Herbert, whose famous autobiography is mentioned on p.53. He was born on 3 April 1593, brought up in Montgomery and was to become a renowned metaphysical poet and hymn writer. His contemporary and friend John Donne visited Montgomery in the spring of 1613 where he was inspired to write his poem 'The Primrose, being at Montgomery Castle, upon the hill, on which it is situate'. George Herbert eventually forsook his noble background to take up holy orders and serve as a parish priest at the village of Bemerton near Salisbury. He died of consumption aged 39 years and was buried there on 3 March 1632.

John Davies Knatchbull Lloyd was born in 1900 into a family who had lived in Montgomery since the early years

UPON this Primrose hill,
Where, if Heav'n would distil
A shower of rain, each several drop might go
To his own primrose, and grow Manna so;
And where their form, and their infinity
Make a terrestrial Galaxy,
As the small stars do in the sky:
I walk to find a true Love; and I see
That 'tis not a mere woman, that is she,
But must, or more, or less than woman be.

Yet know I not, which flower
I wish; a six, or four;
For should my true-Love less than woman be,
She were scarce anything; and then, should she
Be more than woman, she would get above
All thought of sex, and think to move
My heart to study her, and not to love;
Both these were monsters; since there must reside
Falsehood in woman, I could more abide,
She were by art, than Nature falsified.

Live Primrose then, and thrive
With thy true number five;
And women, whom this flower doth represent,
With this mysterious number be content;
Ten is the farthest number; if half ten
Belong unto each woman, then
Each woman may take half us men;
Or if this will not serve their turn, since all
Numbers are odd, or even, and they fall
First into this, five, women may take us all.

Poem 'The Primrose, being at Montgomery Castle, upon the hill, on which it is situate' by John Donne

of the seventeenth century, when they appear in both borough and church records as tanners in the town. They had always played a significant role in the affairs of the borough since one Maurice Lloyd was Bailiff in 1686/7. A few generations later, the Rev. Maurice Edward Lloyd was Rector of Montgomery from 1794 to 1830. His descendent, 'J.D.K.', as he was affectionately known, was a great researcher and recorder of all things relating to his beloved town, contributing over fifty papers to the *Montgomeryshire Collections.* The

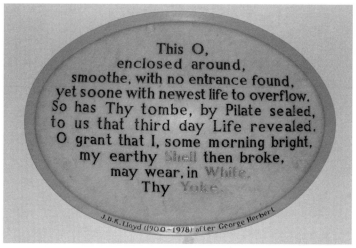

The memorial plaque in the Lymore transept dedicated to the memory of Dr. J.D.K. Lloyd: 'An Easter Egg' a poem written by Dr. Lloyd after the style of George Herbert

publication of this book would have been well nigh impossible without recourse to the many documents written in his own distinctive, but nearly indecipherable, spidery handwriting. He was secretary and chairman of the Powysland Club for many years and served the town as mayor, magistrate, churchwarden and lay reader. The achievement, however, which perhaps gave him most satisfaction, was when he entered and won the modest prize of £5 in a competition in the *Spectator,* for writing a poem with an Easter theme in the style of George Herbert. A year or two before his death, which occurred in December 1978, he sent many of his friends an Easter Card containing the poem, and they reciprocated by placing a tablet containing the poem on the wall of the Lymore transept as a fitting memorial.

On the floor of the Lymore transept close to the Herbert Tomb are two medieval effigies, the identification of which has given rise to much debate. There is a suggestion that the earlier, smaller figure is that of Sir Edmund Mortimer, Shakespeare's 'Revolted Mortimer', subsequent son-in-law of Owain Glyn Dwr and brother-in-law of Hotspur—Henry Percy. The Mortimer family were at one time the most powerful in the land; Sir

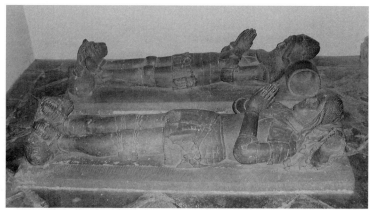

Two effigies in the Lymore transept. The smaller figure is almost certainly Sir Edmund Mortimer d.1408 and the larger, Sir Richard Herbert d.1534, the grandfather of Richard of the adjacent large canopied tomb

Drawing of the Chancel Screen, originally from Chirbury Priory,
by Rev. John Parker from Llanmerewig, dated 1831

Print published by Robert Owen of Welshpool showing the old box pews and pulpit before the major
refurbishments in 1875. The restored east window can be seen and the print must therefore have
been drawn and published between 1859 (the date of the insertion of the window)
and 1875 (the date of Street's restoration of the interior)

Watercolour of the church showing the first tower, by an unknown artist, c.1790

Edmund who died in 1408 was High Constable of Montgomery Castle. The other monument is most probably the effigy of Sir Richard Herbert, grandfather of the Richard of the large canopied tomb. He died in1534, and although the figure appears to date from 1500, it may have been made for him before his death—a not uncommon practice.

The church has been adapted and improved by successive generations in accordance with their ideas of what was fitting, and the needs of the congregation of the time. The most drastic reshaping of the interior of the church however was undoubtedly that which took place in the late nineteenth century. In 1875 the rector and wardens employed a distinguished consultant architect, George Edmund Street (1824-81). He made a series of recommendations, which resulted in the floor level being lowered, and the replacement of the ancient box pews by the present oak pews. It was seen as wrong, in an era of almost universal church attendance, that so much of the seating in church should be in the form of private box pews, leaving insufficient free seating to accommodate the population of the town.

There are a number of additions to the medieval church. In 1816 the present tower was built at the north end of the north transept to replace the old, considerably shorter one, which had become unsafe. The vestry was added between 1830 and 1850, and the present porch dating from 1868 replaced a closed structure with steps outside leading to the upper floor housing the vestry or schoolroom. The new tower cost £1,700 and was paid for by The Right Hon. Edward Herbert Viscount Clive of Lymore, who also financed the enlargement of the Town Hall in 1828.

Buttermilk and Flummery
Say the Bells of Montgomery.
Stay let it Cool
Say the Bells of Welshpool.

An old Montgomeryshire Jingle

The six bells in the tower are all inscribed:

1st bell	Peace & Good Neighbourhood A.R - 1724
2nd	God Preserve the Church of England AR
3rd	Revd M E Lloyd Rector, J Jones & E Read CW Briant Hertford Fecit 1814
4th	Edw Weaver & Fra Greatbach CH Wardens - 1724
5th	John Greenley Esq & Maurice Lloyd Gt Baylifs - 1724
6th	I to the Church the living Call & to the Grave do summon all - 1724

There were fairly strict guidelines laid down regarding the behaviour of the Bellringers:

Rules for 2nd Church Ringers

1   That in addition to the regular Church Ringers certain others not more than eight in number being Churchman be recognised as Church Ringers.

2   That they be appointed by the Rector and Church Wardens and be subject to such rules and regulations as the Rector and Church Wardens from time to time may provide.

3   That a leader be appointed with authority in the belfry and that a secretary be elected.

4   That no one besides those thus appointed be allowed to be in the belfry at the time of ringing except by special permission of the leader.

5   That the Ringers be not entitled to any share of the payments at present received by the old Ringers for services rendered.

6   That they be at liberty to use the bells on two nights in the week (the same being agreed upon & fixed) between the hours of 7.30 and 9 o clock PM provided always and in all cases that these times do not interfere with the times or occasions when the old Ringers have been accustomed or have any special engagement to ring.

7   That in the event of any of the Ringers leaving the parish or ceasing to be a Churchman or being guilty of any immoral or improper conduct he should no longer be a Ringer.

8   That no beer or liquor of any kind on any pretence whatsoever be brought into the belfry and that no smoking be allowed therein.

9   That these Ringers shall have bylaws similar to those of the old Ringers with respect to fines for offences such as swearing drunkenness or other misbehaviours and also for absence or late attendance.

10   That the handbells belong to the belfry.

11   That the times and place of practice be fixed by the Ringers and that the leader be responsible for the care and safekeeping of the handbells.

However, these rules were not always obeyed and with respect to the handbells, the Rev. Glynne Jones, Rector in 1946, recounted that:

> Years ago the bellringers, who used them for practice used to go carol singing with them. Their rounds included the public houses. One night the ringers became so drunk that, when they were visiting Lymore, they lost them and the next day both bells and music had to be retrieved from hedges and ditches. Mr. Parker, the Rector, told the newly appointed clerk, John Davies to collect them and lock them up: he said that they should never be used for this purpose again.

Florrie Proctor, the organist with the church choir, c.1936
Back L to R.: ? , Ivor Tanner, ? , Bernard Tanner, Mr. Helme,
? , Ronny Ancham, Tom Whittingham, Les Evans
Front L to R: Tom Davies (Phil Price's brother),
Charlie Richards, David Jones, Florrie Proctor,
Buster Trow, ? , Turnbull

Before the organ was installed in the church in the nineteenth century, a small band would have provided the music to accompany the singing. One of the instruments was a bassoon and within living memory this was kept in a glass case in the vestry. It is now on display in the Old Bell Museum.

There are a number of interesting graves in the churchyard, the most famous of these being the Robber's Grave. The story of this man buried here who was unjustly hanged has always been a source of fascination. An early account published by the Rev. Mostyn Pryce of Gunley in 1852 changed the names of the characters concerned and embellished the story in the highly romantic style fashionable at that time. The case was subsequently carefully researched by Dr. J.D.K. Lloyd and in an article published in 1961[2] he gave a full account based on information from the gaol files at the Public Record Office and local newspapers of the time:

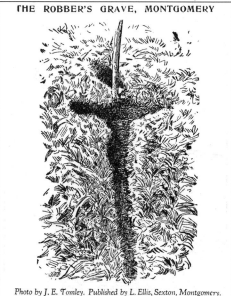

THE ROBBER'S GRAVE, MONTGOMERY

Photo by J. E. Tomley. Published by L. Ellis, Sexton, Montgomery.
Here repose the remains of a man named John Newton, who was hung at Montgomery in 1821 for the crime of Highway robbery. In token of his innocence, Newton asserted that "The grass, for one generation at least, will not cover my grave."

The execution was marked by an appalling outburst of the elements—a fearful darkness spread around, lightning flashed with terrific vividness and thunder rolled in awful majesty.

The sterile cross shown in the photograph marks to this day the fulfilment of the doomed man's prophecy. (COPYRIGHT)

Postcard picture of the Robber's Grave

Gravestone of Gaoler John Davies and his wife

In 1821 John Davies, a slaterer from Wrexham, was accused by William Jones, a labourer employed by Mr. Pugh of Wernllwyd, of assaulting and robbing him of a watch worth thirty shillings and fivepence in coppers. He was found guilty and sentenced to death by hanging. Many people at the time heard the condemned man, either at the trial or at the place of execution, or both, declare his innocence and pray to God that no grass should grow on his grave for a generation as a sign of his innocence. At the moment of the execution there was a violent storm with thunder, lightning and rain, which further convinced bystanders of the truth of his claim. Interestingly, in the same issue of the *Salopian Journal* that carries the account of the execution, the weather report for that day mentions this storm. His grave remained bare of grass for at least a century.

Amongst other interesting memorials is a stone near the porch recording the death, in 1812 aged eighty-four, of another John Davies, 'Keeper of the Goal in this Town' and of his wife Ann, 'Wife of the Keeper of the Goal in this Town', in 1824, aged fifty-seven years. Nearly opposite the west end of the church, is a white marble stone which records the death of P.C William Davies in 1903, aged forty-three years. Carved on the stone are his policeman's helmet, lantern, truncheon and belt.

Until the last century Montgomery, though in Wales, was part of the English Diocese of Hereford. When the Church in Wales became a separate body in the 1920s, parishes such as Montgomery, lying close to the border, were given the option of staying with their English dioceses, or moving into a Welsh diocese. Montgomery is now part of the Diocese of St. Asaph.

View of the church from the west with gardens in the foreground

Chapels

Dissenter chapels appeared somewhat later in Montgomery than in many other Welsh communities. This may well have been due to its position so close to the English border and so far from the early centres of the nonconformist movement. Eventually, four chapels were built. Two were built by the Calvinistic Methodists, the first in 1824, and its replacement in 1885 by what is now the Presbyterian Church in Princes Street. The Wesleyan chapel at the lower end of Arthur Street was founded in 1863 and the Baptist chapel was built in 1900 at the bottom of School Bank. Although there is a wealth of fascinating information concerning the early days of the Calvinistic Methodist movement in Montgomery it has been disappointingly difficult to uncover much of similar interest concerning the other two chapels.

The Calvinistic Methodist Church or Presbyterian Church of Wales

In December 1813, at the Monthly meeting of the Calvinistic Methodists in Llanidloes, discussion took place about attempting to reach the 'neglected populace on the borders of Offa's Dyke', and it was decided 'that it would prove beneficial if we could commence religious services at or near Montgomery say in Mrs. Hamer's house'. It has not been possible to identify Mrs. Hamer or where she lived. Montgomery was probably chosen as it was the county town and the only one of the six county boroughs without a nonconformist meetinghouse. No action would appear to have been taken, for in July 1816 at a meeting held at Llanwyddelan, the Brethren were reminded of their 'resolution to seek a place to preach at Montgomery', but later, in October, it was 'agreed not to go to Montgomery for a while until we see plainer how to proceed'.

At about this time, David James arrived in Montgomery to become the new manager of the tanyard, whose owners, the Lloyd family, had for many years been very strongly involved with the established church. His wife, Elizabeth, was a sister to one of the well-known leading spirits of Welsh nonconformism, the charismatic preacher, Humphrey Gwalchmai of Llanidloes, and it wasn't long before the couple were being encouraged to make efforts to establish the movement in Montgomery. As secretary of the North Wales Association of the Calvinistic Methodist Connexion, Humphrey Gwalchmai had helped draw up the 'Confession of Faith', together with John Elias and John Hughes. One of his copies was written in English to help his sister's work in Montgomery where very little Welsh was spoken.

In the year 1820, Mr. John Maddox, an 'Independent', also lived in Montgomery and he joined the newly arrived couple in starting services in a disused malt house at the back of the Buck Hotel (now T'yr Carw) in Princes Street. The meetings were Calvinistic one Sunday and Independent the other. Encouragingly, at the first services twelve attended in the morning and thirteen in the evening. The arrangement worked well. The untimely death of John Maddox in 1823 was a great loss to the movement, but it was an even greater loss to the Independents for the church henceforth became solely Calvinistic Methodist.

The services soon were to become very popular and in a short time the partition in the malt house was taken down to accommodate the increasing numbers. After three years, the building was required for another purpose by the owner and the brethren received notice to quit. Another meeting place had to be found, and David and Elizabeth James opened the door of their own home to the newly founded congregation. It was no small matter, however, to support the 'Dissenting Cause' in these early days, and the story goes that early on the Monday morning, following the first meeting, the James' saw the landlord coming towards the house and their hearts sank, fearing that he was coming to order them to leave. Mrs. James went forwards to meet him. 'Good-morning Mrs. James', he said, 'I hear that you had a religious service in your house yesterday, and I have come to say that I feel quite vexed because I had not put a proper scraper at your door for the people must have dirtied your room very much'![3] It was very obvious, none the less, that the expanding congregation needed a place of their own.

A lady by the name of Mrs. Lowe offered a plot of freehold land for the purpose of building a new chapel. Unfortunately, this was situated too near to the parish church, and the rector objected on the grounds that his services would be interfered with, but he did, however, promise to help secure a more suitable site for a chapel. The land offered was opposite the eventual position of the new National School and was let at a rental of 10 shillings per annum. The Chapel was built at a cost of £230, and opened on Christmas Day 1824, the officiating minister being the Rev. John Hughes of Liverpool.

A number of factors accounted for the success of the chapel during this period. Foremost amongst these was the establishment of the Sunday School. In the 1820s such a thing as a Sabbath School was unknown in the county town. Surprisingly in those days, when there was usually such antipathy between the established church and the nonconformists, the rector of the parish, the Rev. Maurice Lloyd, seems to have favoured the project as he offered to supply the scholars of the new Sabbath School with bibles and testaments.

The Sabbath School was a great success. In 1850 the number of scholars was 86, increasing to 116 in 1860 and rising further to 190 by 1887, many of the scholars not being members of the chapel. It is important to understand that Sabbath Schools in those days provided not just an introduction to the scriptures but enabled people of all ages, in particular the labouring classes, whose formal education had been lacking, to gain knowledge in a wide range

The first Presbyterian Chapel built in 1824, later to become the chapel schoolrooms and then a private house

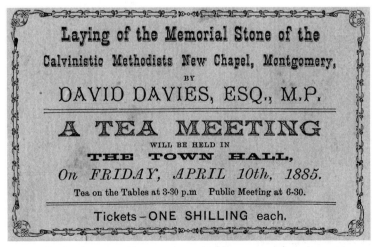

Records of attendance at the Sabbath Schools in the upper division of the English District of the Presbyterian Church of Wales in 1872

of subjects including History, Astronomy, Geography and Science to name but a few.

The chapel attendances grew so rapidly that in a report presented to the Association —the governing body of the Presbyterian Church of Wales—as early as 1875, The Rev. E. Powell and Mr. Newell stated:

The Chapel at Montgomery is unworthy of the Church and congregation. The site is bad.

A later report by Mr. Rowlands of Newtown in 1882, recorded that:

The friends are in need of a new Chapel, for the present one is old fashioned and not worthy of the town nor the connexion. This church keeps up its accustomed good character for liberality and faithfulness. Also the spirit of harmony animates the whole Church and the friends are of good faith that they will before long secure an eligible site.

Laying of the Memorial Stone of the
Calvinistic Methodists New Chapel, Montgomery,
BY
DAVID DAVIES, ESQ., M.P.
A TEA MEETING
WILL BE HELD IN
THE TOWN HALL,
On FRIDAY, APRIL 10th, 1885.
Tea on the Tables at 3-30 p.m   Public Meeting at 6-30.
Tickets—ONE SHILLING each.

Ticket for the Tea meeting following the laying of the Memorial Stone of the new Calvinistic Methodist or Presbyterian Church of Wales in 1885

Eventually a new site was procured in Princes Street, and on Friday 10 April 1885, the memorial stone was laid by David Davies Esq., M.P., of Llandinam. In the cavity of the memorial stone were placed copies of the *Confession of Faith, Monthly Tidings,* the *Oswestry Advertiser,* and the *Montgomeryshire Express.*

The chapel was built of local stone with its front elevation towards Princes Street and was opened with services on Tuesday and

Wednesday, 10 and 11 November 1885. The building with its raked floor looked attractive, both inside and out, and was to became a prominent landmark in the development of the movement, which grew steadily both in membership and influence.

Numerous activities were organised by the chapel at the turn of the century. There are records of grand fund raising bazaars lasting two days, Sabbath School treats and trips to Aberystwyth, picnics and tea parties, concerts and choral festivals.

Postcard view of the Presbyterian Church showing a half-timbered house which was demolished when the manse was built

Mr. Edward Rees James, a nephew of the Rev. Humphrey Gwalchmai continued the family tradition and gave great service to the movement. Born in 1832, he served as Treasurer of the Presbytery and for forty-six years he filled the office of superintendent of the Sabbath School. In addition he was an Alderman of the county council, a county magistrate, and four times Mayor. To quote from *The Treasury*—the monthly magazine of the Calvinistic Methodists—of April 1903:

The Sunday School enjoying their visit to Aberystwyth, c.1910

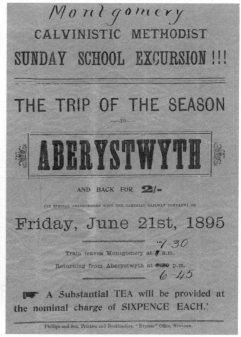

Poster for the Sunday School excursion to Aberystwyth in 1895

The secret of his strength lay in the quiet sincerity of his character. In business his honesty was proverbial his word credit enough. He was trusted as few are. On market days his house resembled a solicitor's office, for his advice was sought after by all sorts of conditions of men. It is the very qualities which had made him such a successful business man that he exhibited as a church worker—prudence sanctified and common sense hallowed by grace.

He died in 1904, in his seventy-second year and the long and detailed report of his funeral in the *Montgomeryshire Express* of 25 October starts as follows:

Wednesday last saw the ancient town of Montgomery shrouded in gloom and depression. The blinds in every house were respectfully lowered and at 11-30 the solemn tolling of the minute bell vibrated through the town, calling the last earthly remains of a good and faithful servant to their last resting place in the old churchyard.

According to his wishes, no service was held in the church or chapel, the coffin being simply borne from the house, on the corner of Broad Street and Arthur Street, to the grave. Along the route, the long solemn funeral cortege led by a posse of police and the fire brigade followed by the mace bearers, family, friends, associates and civic dignitaries from all over the county and from all walks of life, was witnessed by the great majority of the townspeople, who stood 'with uncovered heads and sad hearts'.

Corndon Magazine 1895 (Church Monthly):

Montgomery was early astir on Friday, July 12th, the day fixed for the Sunday School Treat, and Choir and Bell Ringers outing. Smoke was seen issuing out of many a chimney by 4 a.m. and between 6 and 7 large numbers, young and old, were on their way to the Station, some on foot, others in wagons kindly lent by Messrs Stephen and Reuben Davies. Excellent train arrangements had been made by Inspector Gough and Mr. Edwards, Stationmaster. Contingents came from Clun, Forden, and other places for the general public were cordially invited to join the Excursion. The Special left for Aberystwyth at 7-40 with upwards of 400 happy souls out for a holiday, and arrived there at 10 a.m. The youth of Montgomery were soon on the beach, and with a rough sea, and the tide coming in many of them must have got a good soaking, but none seemed the worse for it. The fresh breezes of Aberystwyth are always conducive to good appetites; the important work of catering for the large party was entrusted to the Misses Powell, Darkgate Street. The Sunday School Teachers, Choir and Bell Ringers had dinner at 12 and tea at 4-30 in a large room over the Market. The members of the Sunday School and their friends had tea at 2-30; the rest of the afternoon was spent in various amusements till 6 o'clock, when more refreshment was dispensed and we were off for Montgomery before 7, arriving at the Station by 9. Everyone seemed very pleased with the day, the weather, a most important feature, being all that could be desired. The wagons conveyed the little ones back and all reached home safe and sound, though doubtless tired, having thoroughly enjoyed to many of them the first 'nine hours by the sea-side'. We take this opportunity of thanking those who kindly subscribed towards defraying the expenses of the Treat.

Edward Rees James's funeral cortege processing from his home on the corner of Arthur Street along Broad Street to the churchyard in 1904

Edward Rees James had seven children, three of whom died in infancy and one aged thirteen years. The two remaining daughters, Miss Annie and Miss Mary, continued the family commitment to the chapel. They never married, but devoted their lives to bringing up their late brother, Edward William James's four children: Mary, Rees, Ann and Clara.

Mary Reed (née James), the eldest, wrote down her memories in 1982:

All three chapels flourished when I was a child. Morning and evening services were well attended; everyone dressed in Sunday best, ponies stabled at 'Bevan's yard' next to the chapel, and the traps standing by. In the afternoon on Sunday, the Sunday School was packed with people of all ages, and all in classes with a teacher. Many of the country people came home for tea and then went to the evening service. They were very keen on education and my great aunt and uncle donated a wonderful library to the Sunday School (I read Anthony Trollope in those days!) A good sermon was of great importance, and for this reason preachers went around the churches in turn and families provided hospitality from Saturday night to Monday morning, so that the smallest, poorest chapel could have one of the best preachers in turn. A small, back bedroom in Plas Offa was known as 'the Minister's room'.

The text of a sermon was very important too—and you were expected to remember this, and people would talk about Harvest Thanksgiving sermons years

Bevan's Yard, next to the Presbyterian Church where the ponies of country folk were stabled during Sunday services

after they were delivered. They were tremendous orators and great actors (my husband was terrified the first time he heard one of the sermons in Montgomery over forty years ago!).

The Montgomery Cause seemed to progress reasonably well, but in many parts of the country there was persecution. My father's maternal grandmother was married to a farmer at Timberth [near Montgomery]. All her brothers went to America because it was impossible for a dissenter to buy a farm, or get work on one.[4]

As time passed, the historic difference between the traditions of worship in the Church and the Chapel no longer caused division. Increased understanding and respect led to a desire for greater unity. Joint services became commoner during the second half of the twentieth century and in every activity came an underlying emphasis on the importance of the faith that was to be shared.

Watercolour of the lower part of the town showing the early Wesleyan Chapel prior to the building of the schoolroom. The artist, Mr. Salter of Victoria Buildings and later of Oak Shop, Broad Street, was also a cello player. His wife was the infants teacher at Montgomery School in Mr. Tipping's day

The Methodist or Wesleyan Chapel

The date when the Methodist movement started in the town is not known, but an article in the *Methodist Recorder*[5] in 1909 implies its beginning was low key: 'Methodism in Montgomery had a small and inauspicious beginning, beneath the roof of a godly cottager'. The celebrated preacher and hymn writer Thomas Olivers, is on record as having preached in Montgomery in 1753. Born in Tregynon in 1721, he spent his youth in Forden and was educated at a school in Chirbury. It would appear that

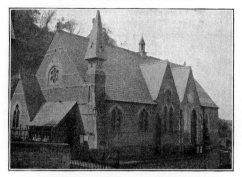

MONTGOMERY WESLEYAN
CHURCH BAZAAR . . . .   **JUNE, 1906.**

A Treasury of . .
Wit and Wisdom

THOUGHTS, WISE & OTHERWISE,
COLLECTED BY

Miss LOUIE DANIELS,   Miss RHODA OWEN,
Miss ADA M. WILLIAMS,
Miss NELLIE REX,   Miss LUCY PRYCE,
Miss MAUD GRIFFITHS,   Miss ANNIE ROBERTS.

PHILLIPS, TYP., NEWTOWN.

A Treasury of Wit and Wisdom
*published for the Montgomery
Wesleyan Church Bazaar in
June 1906. The cover shows the new
schoolroom extension built in 1903*

the somewhat sporadic services were held in private houses, 'old John Whittingham's' being used for a long period of time. The followers did not have an easy time; preachers were occasionally 'hooted and driven from the town' and one evening, in the course of a sermon in a cottage, 'either a cat or a goose was sent down the chimney to disturb'.

Around 1840 during the Chartist riots, the military were quartered in the town using the Town Hall for their barracks and Broad Street for a drilling ground. One of their number, Sergeant Mills, was renowned for his sermons and preached frequently. Whenever he was in the pulpit the room was crowded, many of the soldiers themselves coming to hear their sergeant 'spout'. An orchestra of two violins and a cello provided the music.

In 1862, after many 'fightings without and fears within' it was decided to build a chapel, and a plot of land on the main thoroughfare at the bottom of Arthur Street was secured upon which the chapel with 'accommodation for 200 hearers', was built. The memorial stone was laid in 1863 and the opening ceremony took place in 1864. The cost of the building was £700. By 1900 more room was needed and the *Montgomeryshire Express and Radnor Times* reported in February 1900:

On Monday tea was given to the children attending the Montgomery Wesleyan Sunday School. After which they received the prizes. At 7.30 a meeting was held to consider the proposed building of a schoolroom, which was needed ... followed by a collection being made to the building fund.

By 1903 the extension was completed.

As time went by in the twentieth century, the congregation gradually decreased until only two or three loyal families supported the chapel. Services became more and more infrequent. The last service was held there in 1974 and in 1979 it was sold into private hands.

The Baptist Chapel

The date of the establishment of the Baptist movement in Montgomery is also uncertain, but there are several newspaper reports towards the end of the nineteenth century of services being held in the Town Hall and of annual concerts and bazaars. There are also reports of baptisms in Lymore Pool. The *Montgomeryshire Express and Radnor Times* for Tuesday 26 April 1898 notes that:

> The ceremony of Baptism by immersion was performed at Lymore Park on Sunday afternoon in connection with the Baptist Chapel. A large number of people assembled on the lower pool where the candidates, four in number, were baptised by the Rev. C.P. Thomas, the new pastor of the Baptist Church at Montgomery. An address was given by the Rev. T.E. Williams, Newtown and other ministers assisted at the open-air service, which was held.

At the turn of the century, a meeting was held in the Town Hall where it was agreed that the movement required a permanent home and plans to build a chapel were discussed. There followed a very large bazaar in June 1900 that lasted two days with the object of raising the funds required. A site at the bottom of Princes Street had been purchased and Messrs. Shayler and Edmunds had prepared plans for the building. The funds needed were £1,700—of which the bazaar raised £70. Donations from other sources enabled work to get under way and in November 1900, six memorial stones were laid. After the foundation service, a tea meeting was held in the Calvinistic Methodist schoolroom and in the evening a large congregation attended a service in the Town Hall. Built over an old cesspool, the site was far from ideal and as can be seen from the photograph, the building of red and yellow Ruabon bricks needed to be buttressed to prevent its collapse.

The Baptist 'cause' in Montgomery was not to last long and services ceased before the Second World War. The building was used as a store during the war by the Ministry of Food, after which it was neglected, fell into disrepair and was demolished in 1966. Only the neighbouring manse survives.

The Baptist Chapel built in 1900 at the lower end of Princes Street, overlooked the Pound.
It was demolished in 1966

4　Civic Life

On 15 February 1227, King Henry III granted the first royal charter to the burgesses of Montgomery:

> Know ye that we have willed and granted that our town of Muntgomery be a free Borough for ever. We have also granted that our Burgesses of the said Borough and their heirs that they may enclose their Town of 'Muntgomery' with a ditch and a wall, and that they may have a merchant gild with a hanse and other customs and liberties pertaining to a gild, and that no one who shall not be of that gild shall trade in the aforesaid Borough without the consent of the said Burgesses.

From thence the town was governed by the burgesses with two bailiffs at their head—the High Bailiff and the Low Bailiff, who they elected annually at Michaelmas. All the affairs of the town, including the parliamentary vote, were in their hands. The charter required the burgesses to appoint provosts to keep the town secure and to administer justice to all.

The rights of the burgesses, later to become known as freemen, are hereditary and jealously guarded. Every son of a hereditary burgess is entitled to admission on attaining the age of twenty-one. Widows of the burgesses are, whilst resident in the borough, and so long as they do not remarry, entitled to their late husband's share in any emoluments (see below); but no rights whatever can be transmitted through females. A son of anyone created an honorary burgess can only succeed to his father's rights if he has been born subsequent to his father's admission.[1]

All admissions were originally recorded in the Court Books, which have survived from the first half of the seventeenth century. In practice the control of admission of the burgesses seems to have been vested in the bailiffs and burgesses themselves and at different times in their history, the rights and qualifications for admission appear to show considerable variation.

In 1583 it was ordered that 'no one be admitted a Burgess unless he paid £5 before he was sworn'. In 1654, thirty-two people 'in no way prejudiced unto the corporation', were admitted to be burgesses. The condition of admission of one of the petitioners in 1664 was that he should 'give a long ladder to the use of the town before he should be sworn'. In 1665 and 1667, persons who had married burgesses' daughters were admitted. In 1780 the order was confirmed at the Court Leet that 'no person shall be made a Burgess of this Corporation unless he is entitled to it by birthright or pay the sum of £60 to the Bailiffs for the use of the Burgesses of this Borough'. There are entries in 1670 when several were admitted on petition and several without. In 1689 Hugh Bird, Nathaniel Williams and Richard Gittins were admitted burgesses on Lord Herbert's recommendation, 'because there were so few resident Burgesses'.[2]

Under the Municipal Corporation Act of 1885 all rights of the burgesses (such as the sole right to vote at elections etc.) were swept away and the government of the town was vested in an elected Mayor and Corporation comprised of two aldermen and six councillors, the aldermen being elected by the other councillors. Although the old burgesses and their direct male descendants were deprived of their power and duties they still retained possession of a few acres of low lying land near the railway, known as the 'Fflôs' or Flos. The rent from this is still divided twice a year amongst all resident burgesses over the age of twenty-one years. The two mace-bearers, or sergeants-at-mace, continue to be recruited from the hereditary freemen.

In the seventeenth century the proceeds from the Flos lands were commonly applied to public needs. The Court Leet records show that in 1650 in the Account of Richard Davies, Bailiff, receipts include those 'from Collectors of the Flos amounting to £4 paid in repairs of Hall, Jail and Market House, Pound and Stocks and Hall windows', and in 1654 in the Account of Hugh Price, Bailiff: 'Received from the Flos £1 16s.; paid for making gaol clean, draining gaol and mending stairs and glass in hall, and moss for hall and straw for gaol'. In 1675 it was agreed that 'Common Hall to let ... edgrow of ye flose for foure years for raising money in paying off debts for ye said towne and repairing ye Town Hall, now in much decay, and other necessities'.[3]

Drawing of the Town Hall (built in 1748) by Rev. John Pridden in 1784. Reproduced by kind permission of the National Library of Wales

Early photograph of the Town Hall showing the ground floor open arches where the market was held, and the original clock

The original Town Hall, sometimes referred to as the Guildhall, was sited in the centre of Broad Street and is clearly shown in the small town plan in John Speed's 1610 map of Montgomeryshire (see p.4). This, no doubt, would have been a half-timbered building with an open lower storey similar to that still standing in Llanidloes. In 1748, the much needed new town hall was designed and built at the west end of Broad Street by William Baker from Audlem in Cheshire. He was also involved in the construction of the Butter Cross in Ludlow and the Infirmary in Shrewsbury. The Rev. John Pridden, a traveller and amateur architect, sketched the building in 1784, providing the earliest visual record there is.[4] It shows two storeys, the upper part resting on open arches enclosing a sheltered area for the use of the market. The original upper floor was considerably lower than the present one and eventually found to be inadequate for holding the Quarter Sessions, and in 1828 this was taken down, rebuilt and the roof raised to its present height. The Right Hon. Edward Herbert, Viscount Clive of Lymore generously funded the work. At the same time the rounded rear extension to the building was added, whilst a further addition in the 1930s provided a retiring-room above for the magistrates and room to

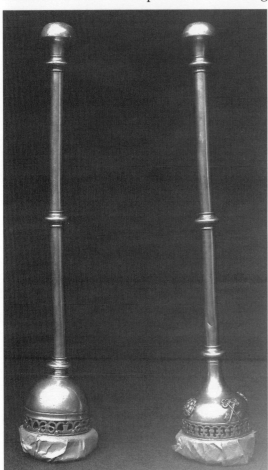

The handsome silver maces are thought to be the second oldest in Wales

house the fire pump below. Early photographs show the lower floor with iron railings set into open arches, subsequently closed with glazed windows in the late nineteenth century. The clock tower was erected in 1921 in memory of Alderman Nicholas Fairles Humphreys who had served the Borough as mayor fifteen times and was an Honorary Freeman.

Of the insignia of the borough of Montgomery there remain the two maces, the constable's staff and the mayoral chain.[5] The fine pair of silver maces are the oldest in the county and the second oldest in Wales, probably dating from 1562, the year of the granting of the new charter by Queen Elizabeth I. They were originally used as weapons of defence by the sergeants-at-mace, whose duty it was to protect important visitors or dignitaries. The head of one of them has a large dent, which has been variously accounted for over the years. Mr. C.P. Davies, landlord of the Dragon Hotel in the 1920s and an hereditary burgess and alderman, claimed the damage was done by his father whilst quelling an uproar in the Checkers Hotel, but another burgess, Mr. Llewellyn Davies, maintained that his grandfather, also one of the sergeants, used it on the head of a

The heads of the maces showing their coats of arms

fiery local character, Braddock the tinker, in restoring order at the Montgomery Wakes. Mr. Davies also told of how one mace disappeared in a disturbance at the Bricklayers Arms only to turn up several days later at the bottom of a copper of dirty water. Despite all these adventures, the maces have survived and continue to be borne by the sergeants-at-mace at the Annual General Meeting of the Town Council and other civic ceremonies.

The mayoral chain dates only from 1909 when Nicholas Fairles Humphreys, on his election as Mayor for the eleventh time, presented it to the Borough. The links bear the names and dates of each of the mayors from 1885 on one side and a design of oak leaves and leek on the other. The wooden constable's staff is painted bluish green and is inscribed in gold, 'Montgomery, Constable's Staff'. Near its tip are the Borough Arms.

Nicholas Watson Fairles Humphreys at Bank House in 1911, wearing the mayoral chain of office, his gift to the Town

Bill Orme, Montgomery's Town Crier in 2000

Local mayors with Nicholas Watson Fairles Humphreys together with their town clerks, including J.E. Tomley, and the macebearers, 1910

There has been little recorded about the early town criers who were almost certainly recruited from the ranks of the burgesses. The Town Crier's bell is engraved as follows:

Borough of Montgomery
Charles Thomas Jones and Robert Jones
Bailiffs in the Year of our Lord 1778

Over recent years, much to the delight of townsfolk and visitors alike, the town's present colourful incumbent can often be seen and most definitely heard in Broad Street on Saturday mornings.

The creation of the county of which Montgomery was nominated the shire town resulted from The Act of Union of 1535-6. The Act brought with it the privilege of Welsh representation in Parliament, and to Montgomeryshire was assigned one member for the county and another for Montgomery Borough. Towards the end of the nineteenth century the Borough seat—which represented

Nicholas Watson Fairles Humphreys receiving the Freedom of the Borough from C.P. Davies on 22 June 1911

Town Council in 1911
L to R seated: Dr. Kirk, C.P. Davies, N. Fairles Humphreys (Mayor), C.B. Williams, Morris Owen.
Standing: Rev. B. Mendis, ? , Rollason, Langford, T.P. Mitchell, ?, ?, ?,
J.E. Tomley (Town Clerk) John Powell, ?, C.S. Pryce, ?, ? .

15th May 1939, Presentation of the Freedom of the Borough of Montgomery to Ald. C.S. Pryce,
Town Clerk 1887-1923, Mayor 1924-1927
Back Row: J.H. Vaughan (Treasurer), F. Hunt (Surveyor), Dr. S.J. Stewart (Medical Officer),
J.E. Tomley, C.B.E. (Financial Officer), L.L. Davies, T.C. Weaver (Freemen) Coun. A.R. Jones
Front Row: Coun. W.H. Gornall, Coun. D. Proctor, The Mayor - J.D.K. Lloyd, Ald. C.S. Pryce,
Coun. T.G. Mitchell, Coun. H.T. Davies.

Newtown, Welshpool, Llanfyllin, Llanidloes, Machynlleth and Montgomery—was fiercely contested between the Tories and Liberals. Two candidates, Sir Pryce Pryce-Jones, Tory, and the Hon. F.S.A. Hanbury Tracy, Liberal, won alternate elections between 1880 and 1892. The electorate in those days was limited to the freemen and householders. Following the election on 8 July 1892 a petition was raised by the Liberals accusing their opponents of malpractice during the campaign. In December 1892, in appalling weather, an exhaustive judicial inquiry was held in the Town Hall. The proceedings, over eight days, received comprehensive press coverage in the local newspapers and daily supplements.[6] The attempts by the English Judges to pronounce the Welsh placenames resulted in much amusement on the public benches, and there were many complaints regarding the lack of accommodation and poor transport facilities from the station. The hearing failed to uncover any misdoing on the part of the Tories. Baron

Ald. C.S. Pryce receiving the Freedom of the Borough from Dr. J.D.K. Lloyd in 1939

The Town Council with Reg Jones as Mayor on the Town Hall steps in 1951, the year he was made an honorary freeman of the Borough

A very early photograph of an election in front of the Town Hall, c.1870. One can see the open polling booths to the left of the building

Pollock and Mr. Justice Wills, who were lodged in the Rectory for the period of the inquiry, were the last Judges to preside over a court in Montgomery. The magistrates' courts continued to be held in the Town Hall until the early 1970s.

In 1974 further changes in local government resulted in the town losing its borough status but retaining an elected Town Council comprising of Mayor and councillors with a very limited budget and much reduced powers.

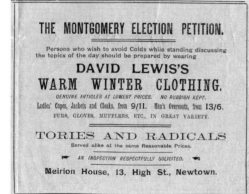

Newspaper advertisements accompanying the reports of the Montgomery Election Petition in December 1892

The declaration of the General Election poll in 1911 behind the Town Hall

5   Lymore Hall

In the sixteenth century, the Herberts were the biggest and most important landowners in the area around Montgomery. They were lords of Chirbury and from 1504, constables of Montgomery Castle. Despite the castle being their main seat, it had been allowed to fall into such disrepair that Lord Edward Herbert, towards the end of his life in 1593, built a large house called Black Hall. Described as a 'low building, but of great capacity', it was almost certainly situated just inside the Town Wall near to Arthur's Gate in the small field between Plas Du and the Cottage Inn. Its life, however, was only short as anecdotal accounts all refer to it as being 'consumed by fire'. By 1623, the Scampions, a family of builders, were busy building a mansion for the Herberts in the middle ward of the castle, which was to become their residence in Montgomery until the Civil War.

After the castle was demolished in 1649 and the previous loss of Black Hall, Lord Edward Herbert the Third Baron of Chirbury complained in a petition to Charles II that he had 'Noe mansion house left him'. In a letter to his brother-in-law, Richard, at Oakeley Park dated 14 January 1673 he wrote that he:

> purposes to build in the Lymore or by Black Hall, as he shall be advised, and to have 300,000 of bricks made the summer following next for the purpose.[1]

'Leymore', as it was referred to in a fourteenth-century document,[2] lay to the south-east of Montgomery. A month or so later, in another letter, he clearly expressed his intention to continue living in or near Montgomery:

> Will sow the whole Frith with nuts and acorns before he [Lord Edward Herbert] is two years older for a perpetual stock of fuel to his family's chief seat, which must be within a mile or two of Mountgomery.[3]

The style of the time was to build a grand house in the countryside surrounded by attractive parkland. There had long been a hunting lodge in the parkland at Lymore and Edward Herbert soon focussed his attentions on this lodge. Before long it was being transformed into a splendid timber-framed mansion, possibly the last great house to be so built in the country. Intriguingly, the style was old fashioned even then, chosen perhaps because of the ready availability of local oak and reusable timbers from other buildings (possibly the castle).

The completion date of the building has usually been regarded as 1675, this being the date which was carved on the centre gable finial together with a coronet and a monogram. It would appear, however, that work continued for quite some time after this. Robert Jones, who was in charge of the building works, reported progress to Lord Herbert in a letter dated 18 February 1677 from Lymore Lodge:

> The carpenters hasten the staircase. The masons continue cutting the earth; a day or two will bring them to the cellar. Tomorrow the stairs to the upper gallery will be all laid, then they'll fall to the arches and partitions. A door is cut into Lord Herbert's dressing room and the other shut up. If he were here he would make his lady's dressing room into a closet, where the bed may be continued, and make the chamber where the 'fellamote' bed is her dressing room (to which there would be a convenient closet under the stairs) and a door into it by the window; which means the hangings will fit, and the same door (will serve) to come out of the gallery into Lord Herbert's whole apartment. The 'paintado' room (the back stairs being taken away) would make a convenient lodging with a closet. This will save charges several ways. This way affords his lady the same prospect.[4]

In 1684, Henry the First Duke of Beaufort (late President of the Council in Wales and Lord Warden of the Marches) journeyed through Wales. One of his escorts was a Thomas Dinely (or Dingley) from Dilwyn in Herefordshire, described as an antiquary. He meticulously recorded the journey in writing and with numerous sketches. Around 20 July he visited Montgomery. Views by Dineley[5] and in the Estate Survey and Valuation of 1785[6] show that the main structure of the Hall changed little throughout its long existence, the building looking much the same as people remember it. The only exception is the roofline where initially there were six small gables (the artist drawing the Estate Survey sketch managed to count eight!). They were altered in the late 1700s to three larger gables as seen in the photographs. The large kitchen block to the right in Dineley's sketch was possibly demolished around the same time.

Sadly, despite its grandeur, the house was rarely lived in for any significant period of time by the Herbert family, being used as a family seat for a period of only seventy-five years, after which it was not occupied by any member of the family.

Henry, the fourth lord, who succeeded his brother in 1678 was

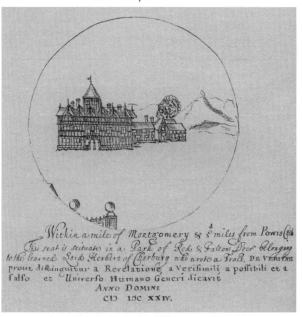

Sketch of Lymore Hall in July 1684 from
The Official Progress of the Duke of Beaufort through Wales in 1684 *by Thomas Dineley, clearly showing six gables*

Engraving of Lymore Hall from the 1785 Survey and Valuation of Lands belonging to the Earl of Powis in the Counties of Montgomery & Salop. *(Note the artist has drawn eight gables!)*

authorised by William III in 1689 to add a fresh unit to the British Army. He set out from Lymore on 19 March to enlist the required number of troops for the new regiment. Within a short time this was accomplished and the Twenty-third Regiment of Foot, later known as the Royal Welch Fusiliers was duly formed. It is not unlikely that, before resigning his command of the regiment, Lord Herbert entertained the officers, together with some of his tenantry who had enlisted, in the spacious dining hall and Burgess hall at Lymore.

Henry died childless in 1691, but his widow, Lady Catherine Newport, a daughter of the 1st Earl of Bradford, continued to live at Lymore. After her death in 1714, the estate passed to her husband's great nephew, Henry Arthur Herbert. It was then that the original manuscript of the *Autobiography of the 1st Lord Herbert of Chirbury* (written 'for the

Lymore Hall from the north. A small part of the long fence in front still remains

Front view of the Hall with a visiting car, and a clear view

instruction of his posterity') was discovered at Lymore amongst a quantity of old papers, in 'a very bad condition'. It once again disappeared only to be rediscovered in a box at Powis Castle some years later. It was privately printed by Horace Walpole in 1764 and is said to be the earliest instance of an autobiography in the English language. The remarkable document recounts his adventures, from his birth to 1624 in an unabashed manner describing his martial valour, success with women, truthfulness, sweetness of breath and other virtues.

Henry Arthur Herbert did not reside permanently at Lymore and the Hall remained unchanged over the years, for it was doubtless considered unnecessary to remodel it in accordance with eighteenth- and nineteenth-century ideas. It was, however, kept in spotless condition with highly polished

The herbaceous border in the walled garden

Water flowed through underground culverts from the upper pool to the lower pool to drive the sawmills in front of Lymore farm buildings

East view of the Hall taken from near the present cricket pitch showing the extensive formal garden with the town in the background

NAMES OF GUNS.

1. H. R. H. Prince of Wales
2. His Grace Duke of Devonshire
3. Marquis of Camden
4. Lord Cecil Manners
5. Capt: B Godrey Faussett
6. Earl of Powis
7.
8.
9.

LYMORE. 1 Day

Beat P. Castle & Rhalt Lymore
Date Nov: 23 24 25 19 09

Pheasants	Cocks ...	
	Hens Phs	2969
Partridges		2
Woodcock		4
Snipe		
Wild Duck		4
Teal		4
Hares		49
Rabbits		55
Various		1
TOTAL ...		3094

Record of the game shot at the Royal shooting party, hosted by the Earl of Powis, on 23, 24 & 25 November 1909. George Baldwin (Arthur Baldwin's father) was then the gamekeeper at Lymore and the card is in his handwriting

oak floors and contained many beautiful articles including Gobelin tapestry wall hangings and fine furniture. During this time its gardens and parterres continued to be meticulously tended in the style of the time when they were first laid out. A succession of agents to the Powis estate resided there and it was used annually for preparing rent rolls, for the Burgesses' Dinner and for shooting parties. The most notable of these was in November 1909 when the Prince of Wales and other members of the Royal family attended a shoot at Lymore.

The Royal shooting party at Lymore, 25 November 1909.
Photograph taken by F.E. Anderson of J.H. Anderson & Son, Welshpool.
The names reading from the left are, top row:
Lord Clive, the Duke of Devonshire, Lord Camden, Capt. Godfrey Foussett, the Prince of Wales,
the Earl of Powis, Sir Donald Mackenzie Wallace, the Hon. Sidney Grevelle, Lord Cecil Manners,
Mr. Forrester Addie, Col. Edward Herbert, C.B.
Bottom row:
Lady Louise Loder, the Duchess of Devonshire, Lady Hermione Herbert, Lady Camden,
the Princess of Wales, Lady Yarborough, Lady Dalhousie, the Duchess of Norfolk, Lady Bradford

Comments from visitors over the last fifty years of its life shed light on the general condition of the great house. T.E. Pryce recorded in 1885:

> ... one peculiarity of Lymore was that whilst the oak floors were so highly polished, the oak stairs were scrubbed to a whiteness seldom seen in more modern days.
>
> Attention should be called to the beauty and variety of the door and window furniture throughout the house. The wrought escutcheons on the windows, and their curious fastenings, are a perfect study, and so is the brass work on the doors; whilst in the State bedroom a key still remains of chased steel of exquisite design and finish.[7]

Fletcher Moss wrote in 1903:

The first floor landing of the Great Staircase

The oak in this house is wonderful. All the floors are waxed and polished, but the panelling, doors and other oaken work is simply dusted, neither oiled nor waxed, and consequently is a light grey colour, very different from the ordinary conventional idea of oak; the floors are beautifully glossy and dark and very slippery, and therefore rather dangerous - the light oak often shows the graining or medullary rays very beautifully, and some of the panels are of immense breadth. The place is certainly very well kept, fires being made in the winter.[8]

In 1929 Mary Newill Owen described her childhood memories of the old house. Her grandfather, Thomas Newill, was Agent to the Earl of Powis and was resident there.[9]

I have visited Lymore for the last time, a house where I spent the happiest days of my life, and it is pleasant to call to memory the long summer days spent in the old house, but not less delightful were the short winter days, when the twilight set in early and the old house was warm and softly lighted by candles and lamps.

Among the great charms of Lymore were the highly polished oak floors, over which, unless you were used to them, one took perilous journeys. They were kept to a brightness of such a degree that you could see the furniture reflected in them, and which with the ruddy glow of the fires in the different rooms produced a particularly cheerful effect, more especially so in the winter as one came in from the outside gloom and saw a beautiful tea table with its gleaming old silver set out in the dining hall.

In those far off days Lymore was furnished with very many beautiful old and valuable specimens of the cabinetmaker's art. Two cabinets, with their secret drawers, were a source of unending delight on a rainy day, for one was always finding some new device of the old world artists to hide documents or treasures in. Both of these old cabinets are now in the oak drawing room at Powis Castle.

An object of childish terror was the full length portrait of Queen Catherine of Braganza, wife of Charles II, which was hung at the foot of the short staircase leading to the white drawing room (now also in the oak drawing room at Powis Castle).

The old hawk pens and the dark and eerie looking rooms leading to the leads have been for many years the abode of a large and flourishing colony of bats. In June 1884, the late Mr. Bailey, the headkeeper at Lymore, and his assistants destroyed upwards of a hundred of these weird creatures which were hanging in clusters from beams in the unused rooms leading from the Minstrel's gallery and others from other parts of the house were dealt with later on. This wholesale massacre of bats was a great joy and relief to those who were staying at Lymore at the time.

Most old houses seem to have attracted the idea that they are haunted in some way. Lymore was no exception, T.E. Pryce in his account of 1885 when describing the State Room recounts:

The foot of the staircase on the ground floor

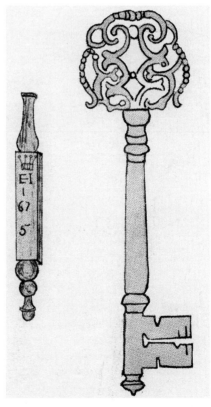

Drawing of the inscription on the central gable, and the key to the State Room (now at Powis Castle)

This room was the scene of an undeniable ghost story. Some years ago a gentleman sleeping here was aroused by strange noises, the bedcurtains shook, the curtain rails rattled, the air seemed alive with weird shapes and sounds; while fitful tappings at the latticed panes, and flutterings against the hangings, proclaimed the presence of the pale shade of Hades. Presence of mind however exorcised the apparition and a lighted candle disclosed the fact that dozens of bats were bent upon colonising the apartment.[10]

Drawing of detail of carving on the staircase and the entrance to one of the bedrooms

By the Light of the Moon was a ghost story published in the *Montgomery County Times* of 6 October 1906. It was based on the actual discovery, in one of the Lymore pools when it was drained in 1860, of a Civil War helmet that still contained a skull. For many years the helmet with its skull and breastplate were to be found on a cabinet in one of the rooms at Lymore. In 1929 it was donated to the Powysland Museum[11] from where, unfortunately, it seemed to have disappeared.

A downstairs room showing the panelling

It has turned up, however, in the Royal Armouries at Leeds, where the Keeper of Armour has recorded its recent history:

> The late fifteenth-century sallet converted into a harquebusier's pot from Lymore Hall has been on loan to us from the Powysland Museum since 1984. Before that it was stolen from the [old] Powysland Museum, and had been converted back into a sallet for sale before it was spotted and recovered. I think the museum felt it was too vulnerable there, and we were happy to take it on loan. It has its seventeenth-century quilted lining (a very rare thing in itself) and its associated skull with it.

Staff group with the Agent outside Brummell's Court (probably the oldest part of the Hall)

The fate of the old house was sealed on a Thursday in August 1921 when a near catastrophe took place, as recorded the following Tuesday, 9 August, in the *Montgomeryshire Express and Radnor Times*:

A Montgomery Sensation

FLOOR COLLAPSES AT CHURCH BAZAAR

A most untoward accident, fortunately unattended by fatal consequences, occurred at the bazaar and fete held at Lymore Hall, Montgomery, on Thursday last. The scene of the accident was the big banqueting hall of the old stately mansion, which for the nonce had been transferred into a brilliant bazaar sale room - a riot of colour, gaiety and animation. The business of the bazaar was in full swing; stalls were being besieged with eager buyers; outside the band was playing, and the number of guests were just crossing from an ante-room after hearing a delightful concert organised by the committee. There was considerable congestion of people near the main entrance of the hall - a laughing, gaily chatting throng. Suddenly, without any audible promonitary symptoms, a knot of guests was observed to disappear outright.

The polished oak floor on which they were seen to stand had disappeared over a space of about twelve feet by six feet. It had all happened almost noiselessly, and those standing in the immediate neighbourhood were for the moment petrified. Even those who had not made this sudden drop of nearly twelve feet into the stone vaults felt very insecure, as other portions of the floor looked very unstable in consequence. The cavity where 17 guests had disappeared was approached with caution, and a ladder being quickly procured through Mr. Reg Jones, a descent was made to see what damage to life and limb there might be. There was slight evidence among those who remained above board, and some of the ladies showed a tendency to faint, because it was feared that very severe consequences had ensued. The Rev. B.J. Phillips, Berriew, who was among those who had made the descent, called up and reassured the anxious people in the hall. The casualty list was happily and unexpectedly very light, considering the serious nature of the mishap. With the people who fell into the vault was the fancy stall over which Miss Doris Tomley presided. The young lady, fortunately, did not accompany her stand in its downward track, but was left standing on the edge of the chasm. The Earl of Powis was at the time talking to the Rector of Montgomery. Lord Powis disappeared, but the rector was left on the solid floor. The Earl escaped with very slight injuries, as also did his agent, Mr J. Edmonds, who when in the depths found himself almost inextricably mixed with the fancy goods of Miss Tomley's stall. The Countess of Powis was only about two yards distant from the subsidence when it occurred, and the Countess D'Arcy was also in close proximity. Altogether 17 disappeared, which included, in addition to those already mentioned, Mr. and Mrs. Lloyd, Castell Forwyn; Mr. Lloyd, although suffering from shock, escaped practically unhurt, but Mrs. Lloyd was severely shaken and is still receiving medical attention; Mrs. Kilvert, a Montgomery lady of over 70, was shaken, but otherwise unhurt; the Rev. D.D. Peirce, Sarn, who sustained bruises to head and hands; Miss Morris, Jamesford, who alighted heavily and sprained both ankles; Mrs. W.V. Davies and Miss Davies, Pentrenant, who escaped any bodily injury. Mr. E. Griffiths, Birmingham, who was on a visit to his home, sustained a minor injury to his leg; Miss Maud Crosse, a lady journalist on the staff of the *Montgomery County Times*, who came out unscathed; Miss Dorothy Davies, domestic servant at the Hollies, who had an ankle sprained; Mabelle Klarigopski, the Russian danceuse, who was none the worse for the fall.

Some of the occupants of the cellar were brought up the ladder, others were conducted through the underground passages to the steps outside the hall. Medical aid was luckily readily available, as Dr. Kirk was present in the hall at the time of the mishap, and Dr. Phillips was soon on the scene. A telephone message also speedily brought Dr. A. Shearer, Newtown, to Plas Trefaldwyn, where he saw to the needs of Mr. and Mrs. Lloyd, who had been taken thither in a car. The other unfortunates were similarly conveyed to their respective homes. Miss Doris Vaughan, a nurse at the County Infirmary, happened to be amongst the guests, and assisted the doctors in their work.

It is rather curious that the floor should have collapsed at this juncture, because on the previous evening a pianoforte weighing almost half a ton was wheeled over this particular spot. The hall itself has not been used as a residence since the death of the late Earl of Powis. It is surprising none the less, with its stout oak timbers, that the floor should have given way.

Needless to say, the proceedings terminated simultaneously with the unlucky collapse. No doubt the promoters will hold a further bazaar later in the season.

The house had not been slept in since 1886 and after this episode no further public functions were held there either, and the house fell into disrepair. After much deliberation the Earl of Powis eventually announced in a letter to the *Daily Mail* in September 1929, that he was obliged to sell the home of his ancestors. A considerable sum of money would be needed to preserve the house, he stated—more than he felt justified in spending. He had offered it to the nation through the Office of Works without success, and concluded that 'since the house contained much valuable oak panelling, a very fine staircase and oak floorboards of considerable beauty and interest it seems folly to allow this to deteriorate and in time become worthless'..

It is said that the Earl of Powis offered Lymore for £1 a year to anyone who would put it in order. No offers had been forthcoming and the sale and subsequent demolition became inevitable.

The architect A.B. Waters surveyed Lymore prior to its sale and described it in the *Montgomeryshire Collections:*

BY DIRECTION OF THE RIGHT HON. THE EARL OF POWIS.

Lymore

MONTGOMERY,

∴ WALES. ∴

Shrewsbury 21 miles. Welshpool 8 miles. Craven Arms 18 miles.

SALE CATALOGUE of the

Historic **Elizabethan Mansion** *including* THE WHOLE OF THE OAK PANELLING, OAK FLOORING, FIREPLACES, MAGNIFICENT ELIZABETHAN OAK STAIRCASE, & ENTIRE STRUCTURE WITH BEAUTIFULLY TIMBERED ELEVATIONS.

HARRODS

are directed by the Rt. Hon. The Earl of Powis, to Sell by Auction, on the Premises, either as a Whole or in Lots (unless sold in the interim), on Friday, October 25th, 1929, at 1.30 p.m.

The Mansion may be Viewed upon production of this Catalogue to the Caretaker-in-charge at the Cottage in the Grounds.

Resident Agent: W. M. MARRIOTT, Esq., Estate Office, Powis Castle, Welshpool.
Architects and Surveyors: Messrs. BODLEY & HARE, 11, Grays' Inn Square, W.C.
Auctioneers: Messrs. HARRODS, Ltd., 62-64, Brompton Road, London, S.W.1, and at Byfleet, Manchester, Le Touquet, and the Riviera.

Frontispiece from Harrods' Sale catalogue of 1929

The north, south and east sides of the house are bounded by gardens, and on the west side is an open courtyard. On the north side there is a lawn with a central path, liberally planted with trees and shrubs and separated from the park by wooden railings. To the south is a small walled enclosure, with double gates opening onto the grassy bank of the Upper Pool. This is known as Brummell's Court, but there is no information as to who Brummell was. To the east is a very fine walled garden, with wide borders and broad grassy walks. Flowers of all descriptions grow in profusion, mingling with old fruit trees and fine yew hedges; unaltered so far as one can judge for the last two hundred years.[12]

The sale of Lymore, with Mr. Robinson-Smith, the manager of Harrods Estate Office as auctioneer, took place on 25 October 1929. It had been thought up till the previous day that the sale might be cancelled, as an offer of £10,000 had been made to the Office of Works through the National Trust for the Preservation of Ancient Buildings, to preserve the mansion for the nation, provided Lord Powis was prepared to give the fabric. Sadly this

Front view of the Hall after demolition had started

The Hall in an advanced state of demolition

was not considered by the Office of Works to be sufficient to put the place in order and for the general upkeep of the house. The sale therefore went ahead as planned in a marquee in front of the house on a Friday afternoon. It did not attract a large number of purchasers, but several prospective buyers travelled many miles to be present. Bidding commenced with an offer of £500, and within five minutes the fittings and fixtures of the entire house, with the exception of those in room 24, which Lord Powis wished to keep for himself, was purchased for £3,600 by Mr. F.E. Anderson, an antique dealer from Welshpool. (Interestingly, it was Mr. Anderson, also a professional photographer, who had taken the official photograph of the Royal shooting party at Lymore twenty years before).

On Wednesday 20 May 1931 Lymore Hall, stripped of all its fittings, was sold in lots for demolition. The great staircase had already found its way to Aldborough Hall in Yorkshire, and much of the remaining timber was purchased for reuse by Major Kenneth Hutchinson-Smith, a builder from Wolverhampton. He still holds a high reputation for his well-designed 'mock Tudor' houses in the Midlands, two of which were given the name Lymore.

The sad pictures of the demolition of Lymore Hall are the last views of what had been a very fine and unique mansion much loved by all who were privileged to know it. Today, all that there is left is a short length of the original wooden fence, beyond which is a tangled jungle of brambles, overgrown box trees and self seeded saplings. It requires considerable imagination to envisage where the grand gardens were laid out and where the old Hall had once stood for over 250 years.

6 Schools

The earliest written record of formal education in Montgomery is of a pre-reformation 'grammar' school in the first half of the sixteenth century. This was attached to the 'Guild' or 'Fraternity of the Blessed Virgin' and financed by the revenue from its lands, one part of which was called 'the Colledge' described as being 'a messuage near the parish church and in the occupation of Henry Sturges, the Rector'.

Under the Chantries Acts of Henry VIII and Edward VI, commissions were set up to enquire into the number, nature and revenues of 'all chauntries, hospitalls, colleges, free chappells, fraternities, brotherhoods, guylds, and salaries of stypendarie priests, within this realm of England and Wales and the Marches'. One of the returns of the commissioners dealt with the guild and its school in Montgomery:

In a contemporary report of the Commissioners, observations were made concerning the Guild and its school:

> The Fraternyte or late Service of our lady in the said Towne.
> Rentes of landes and Tenements, 26s. 9d.
> And vpon the increase and yerelye proffytes of a Stock of
> Cattel preysed to be solde at £330 15s. 4d., £40 . £41 6s. 2d.
> Entre this in the warrant of contynewance.
> Mathew David, Clerc, verie aged and impotent, Stypendary
> prest by the brotherheade seale, £8.
> Allowe hym the yerelie Somme of £6.
> William Ilkes, Clerc, Stipendary prest £8
> Pencion, £4.
> Sir hugh woodes, another stipendarye, 106s. 8d.
> Pencion, £4.
> Rychard Smythe, Orgaynplayer, 100s
> Pencion, 66s. 8d.
> John Elkes, keper of the quyre, being a poor man £4 0s. 8d.
> Allowe hym 40s. yerelie.
> John Bocher and Mathew ap Richard, querysters, eyther of
> them, 13s. 4d . . . . 26s. 8d.
> William ap John, holy water bearer, 6s.

It appearyth by the depositions of the Proctors, wardens and presenters ther, that those same dyd fynde and hiere one prest or lerned man continually, by the space of

30 yeres by past, to keape a free schole in the said Towne, albeit that Sir William Ilkes, above named, beyng cheyfelye hyred for that purpose, taught but yonge begynners onelye to write and syng and to reade soo farre as the accidens Rules, and noo Grammar, sythens the feast of Sainte Michell the archangell last past.[1]

Later, following the demolition of the castle after the Civil War, a Puritan or Free school was founded in 1650. It aimed to educate pupils in Greek and Latin, with the Puritan bias being reflected in the great emphasis laid on the English Bible, and was the first attempt by the state to accept responsibility for the provision of free education. A sixth of the tithes of Wales was devoted to the maintenance of these schools.

Pridden's drawing of the church in 1784 showing the steps to the schoolroom above the porch. Reproduced by kind permission of the National Library of Wales

No further records of this establishment exist and the experiment was probably short lived.

The drawing of the church by Pridden in 1784 shows the steps to the right of the porch leading to an upper room once used as a schoolroom and vestry. This porch was replaced in 1868. Similar examples survive in Guilsfield and Lydbury North churches.

In the early eighteenth century efforts were made to found charity schools within Wales. Those instituted by the nonconformists were very few, although Montgomery was mentioned as one of the towns in which a school was to be set up under the will of the Rev. Dr. Daniel Williams of Wrexham in 1711:

My Will is that they, the Trustees, choose and appoint some pious grave person for to teach twenty poor children to read English and instruct them in the principles of the Christian religion in these following towns, for as long a time as my said Trustees shall think fit and meet, and no longer, viz. Denbigh, Flint, Caernarvon, Montgomery, Beaumaris or else Conway, Merioneth or Holt and Chelmsford.

It appears that the attempt was a failure and that:

The master at Montgomery was harrassed by the Town Warden's *sorry rogue* from Anglesey, who informed the Magistrates 'that there was kept in his Town a Presbyterian school and that the Master did not communicate in the Church of England nor teach the Church catechism and that he had corrupted all the town and the country'.[2]

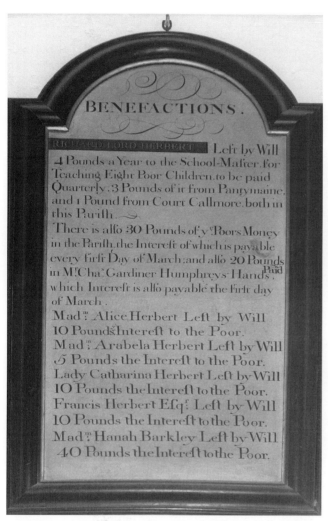

BENEFACTIONS.

RICHARD LORD HERBERT Left by Will
4 Pounds a Year to the School-Master, for
Teaching Eight Poor Children, to be paid
Quarterly; 3 Pounds of it from Pantymaine,
and 1 Pound from Court Callmore, both in
this Parish.
There is also 30 Pounds of ye Poors Money
in the Parish, the Interest of which is payable
every first Day of March; and also 20 Pounds
in Mr Chas Gardiner Humphreys Hands,
which Interest is also payable the first day
of March.
Mad^m Alice Herbert Left by Will
10 Pounds, Interest to the Poor.
Mad^m Arabela Herbert Left by Will
5 Pounds the Interest to the Poor.
Lady Catharina Herbert Left by Will
10 Pounds the Interest to the Poor.
Francis Herbert Esqr Left by Will
10 Pounds the Interest to the Poor.
Mad^m Hanah Barkley Left by Will
40 Pounds the Interest to the Poor.

Benefaction board in the north transept of the church listing some of the legacies left to the poor of the parish and for their education

Local charities were founded which included provision for encouraging the education of the poor, some surviving well into the twentieth century. The Edwards Charity provided, by indenture dated 26 September 1770, '£5 towards the charge of maintaining a schoolmaster, and £2 annually for a school mistress to teach the children of the poor inhabitants of the said parish and town of Montgomery to read, write and cost accounts'. Richard Lord Herbert left, by will, £4 per annum to a schoolmaster for teaching eight poor children, to be paid quarterly.

The arrival of the Nonconformist movement in the early 1800s significantly improved the provision of free education for children and, perhaps more importantly, adults. In the well-attended Sunday Schools, pupils were not only taught the scriptures but also a wide variety of other subjects. The Calvinistic Methodists established a Sunday school in the very early days of the movement in Montgomery collecting a substantial library for its use (see p.35).

From the middle of the 1700s, numerous 'private schools' had appeared throughout the town, many of them located in totally unsatisfactory premises with inexperienced and unqualified teachers. In 1847, the Report of the Commission of Enquiry into Education in Wales[3] provided a comprehensive and detailed study of the state of education in Montgomery with its 1,208 inhabitants. (At that date no National or British school had been established in the town, these being founded by the British and Foreign School Society, and the National Society respectively; see p.69.)

The parish abounds with small private and dame schools [small private schools run by an elderly woman, usually for children of primary school age], of which there are seven in the town of Montgomery and one on the borders of the parish of Forden. A limited number of the poor are taught free in the following schools, partly by individual charity, partly at the expense of certain funds arising from subscriptions and endowment.

Montgomery Free School. - A school for boys and girls, taught by a master, in a room of a dwelling-house. Number of boys, 16; of girls, 11. Subjects taught - the Bible, the Church Catechism, reading, writing, and arithmetic. Salary of master, £27, with house and garden rent free, for which he is required to teach 27 scholars free.

I examined this school April 12, when 18 of the above-mentioned scholars were present, nearly all of whom were above 10 years of age. I found 5 able to read a verse of the Bible correctly, and to answer a few questions upon Scripture history; of the rest, none had any knowledge of the Bible, although 14 could repeat parts of the Church Catechism; only 3 possessed any available knowledge of arithmetic; and only 6 copy-books could be found in the school belonging to children at present members, not one of which contained good writing. No instruction is given to mental arithmetic, in the elements of geography, or in English grammar, although the pupils are in far better position for learning these subjects, from their knowledge of English, than the children in many Welsh schools, where they are taught success-fully, and where the income of the teacher is considerably lower in proportion to the number taught. It appears that the girls receive instruction for only three hours daily, being taught needlework every afternoon in a separate school.

The master has been 30 years engaged in teaching, but has not been trained. He adopts neither the National nor any other specific method of teaching. He is allowed to take an unlimited number of pay scholars, at terms which exclude the poor.

Mrs. Jones' School. - A school for boys and girls, taught together by a dame, in a cottage kitchen. Number of girls, 5; of boys, 9. Subjects taught - reading and the Church Catechism. Total income of mistress £5 12s. 10 scholars are taught free, the rest pay 3d. per week.

I visited this school April 12 but the children were not assembled. The kitchen in which they are said to be taught was dirty and comfortless in the extreme. It contained some dishes, pots, and pans, but no school furniture. The mistress complained bitterly of poverty and illness. Some of her pupils are above 10 years of age. She does not teach needlework. No one assists her to give instruction either in religion or in other subjects. They provide their own books, and choose what they please.

Mrs. Davies's School.- A school for boys and girls, taught together by a dame, in a cottage kitchen. Number of scholars, 25. Subjects taught - the Bible, the Church Catechism, reading and writing. Fees, 11 children at 3d., 7 at 1d. per week; the rest are free scholars and learn needlework only.

I examined this school April 12, when 13 children were present. The kitchen in which they were assembled was not suited for the purpose, being ill lighted and inca-pable of ventilation. It contained no furniture, except a few small forms, and the utensils proper for washing, cooking, and other domestic purposes.

I found only 2 scholars able to read a verse of the Bible, and that incorrectly, and with difficulty; only 3 were learning to write on paper, and their copy-books were illegibly written; 8 repeated parts of the Church Catechism; but their information was exceedingly little on all subjects, especially on Holy Scripture.

The mistress is competent to teach reading and needlework, but has not been trained to conduct a school and has no idea of any system of instruction, or of governing and working a school efficiently.

ABRAHAM THOMAS, *Assistant*

An additional tabular report recorded a total of eight schools and the date when they were established: Montgomery Free School (1747), Mrs. Jones's School (before 1817), Mr. Smith's School (1823), Mrs. Smith's School (1823), The Buck Room School (1833), Mrs. Davies's School (1834), Mrs. Sneade's School (1844), and Caerhowell Lodge School (1845).

Montgomery Free School was housed in the Three Links Hall at the foot of Buck Bank, where it was run by Abraham Bagley. It is almost impossible to identify the location of the other establishments but there are records of schools at the Flower House, Rock House, Country Works Gallery, Myrtle House and Glebe House. In several of these, children's names are scratched on the glass windowpanes. From the census returns it can be seen that some of the schools took in boarders, for example, in 1871 Catherine Statham, 'principal of school' is recorded as living in Broad Street with Martha Lavender, 'assistant mistress', and eight girls and one boy aged between seven and fifteen years as 'boarders'. Many of these children lived on farms too far away to travel daily, particularly in the bitter weather of the winter months.

The 1847 report demonstrated that Montgomeryshire had been neglected in respect of education. Although the schools were not deficient in number they were generally self supported and held in totally inadequate and unsuitable buildings; churches, chapels, shops or cottage kitchens and rarely in a school built for that purpose. The teachers were mainly lacking in training and of poor quality. The voluntary British and Foreign School

School as it was when it was built in 1865 from an early glass plate, c.1905

Society (1808) and The National Society (1811) had been founded in England to promote the education of the poorer child, relying on voluntary subscriptions and school fees. The National Schools were to teach the religious principles of the Church of England. At the time of the report there were only a handful of these schools in the county. During the 1840s and 1850s considerable local social and industrial unrest developed in towns across Montgomeryshire with a growing demand for 'sound and secular education for all'. This added to the increasing demands on the government for a national system of education but it wasn't until the Forster Act of 1870 that they began to accept responsibility for education throughout the country.

Montgomery's National School was established in 1865. The first move towards the building of the school came from the then rector, the Rev. Maurice Lloyd, who approached Lord Powis telling him of the need for a school in Montgomery. He responded by giving three-quarters of an acre of land together with £500 towards the cost of erecting a school building on the site. The Rev. Lloyd himself contributed £100, and the National Society and the Hereford Diocesan Board of Education each gave £50. Many smaller gifts towards the project were received until a sum of £1,110 1s. 10d. was realised. Team labour was offered and supplied by local farmers for the hauling of stone to fence the grounds. The architect of the buildings was Mr. Nicholson of Hereford and the builder, Mr. Gough of Bishop's Castle. The cost was £1,005 and the architect's fee was £65 18s. 10d.

With the work completed by the end of 1864 the school was opened on 13 February 1865, the school managers having appointed Mr. James

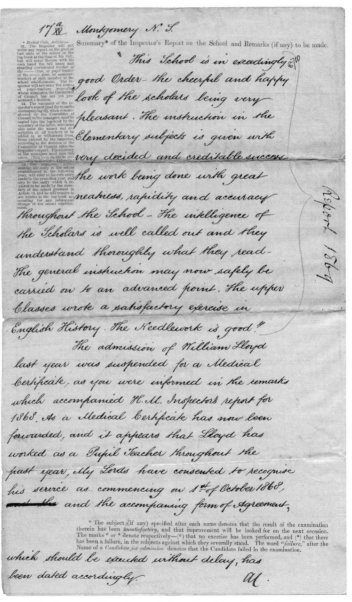

The favourable report of the school inspector in 1869

Early Montgomery school photographs 1881. The school log book entry for 14 July 1881 reads: 'Children photographed in four groups by a travelling photographer. 128 present. Attendance still below the mark on account of haymaking'

Montgomery School photographs in 1902 with Mr. Tipping, headmaster, in the top photograph, which also shows how these were usually mounted. The school log book entry for 14 November 1902 reads: 'The children photographed by Mr. Geo. Holdsworth, Hepworth, Huddersfield'

72

Dash Perkins as the first schoolmaster. Mr. Perkins was assisted by his sister as schoolmistress, and the teaching staff also included a pupil teacher and a school mistress for the infant school.

For the first few years the main cost of supporting the school was borne by voluntary subscribers, but as the years passed government grants increased and the burden of maintaining the school fell less and less upon the parishioners. With the passing of the Education Act of 1902, the State assumed responsibility for the maintenance of the fabric and the payment of the teachers' salaries. Although the school was run by the established church and a significant proportion of the children of school age were from a nonconformist background, there was little evidence of any secular or political conflict to impede its development. Montgomery was almost entirely English speaking and language was never a problem. Small private schools still continued to operate in the town well into the twentieth century.

In Montgomery the official school log books[4] have survived and provide an excellent record of the changing social life within the town. The code of regulations printed in the opening pages start with the following instructions:

> The principal teacher must daily make in the Log Book the briefest entry which will suffice to specify either ordinary progress, or whatever other fact concerning the School or its Teachers, such as the dates of withdrawals, commencements of duty, cautions, illness, &c., may require to be referred to at a future time, or may otherwise deserve to be recorded.
>
> No reflections or opinions of a general nature are to be entered in the Log Book.
>
> The Inspector will call for the Log Book at his annual visit, and will report whether it appears to have been properly kept throughout the year.

James Perkins, the first headmaster, recorded the school's opening:

> These schools were opened with prayer by the Rev. M. Lloyd and the Rev. N. Neville Curate of Montgomery, Mrs. Lloyd and Miss Neville attended to assist my sister in organising the sewing classes.

School routine was soon underway:

February 16   Used corporal punishment for the first time in this school today.

February 17   Many away owing to severe weather. Selected 12 boys and 12 girls to form a choir.

February 28   Rev. N. Neville presented a football to boys.

March 8   New Harmonium for school.

March 13   Punished 2 boys for bad behaviour at Church yesterday.

May 26   Began School at 1. Am going to leave off at 3 and am going to take the boys to a cricket match at Forden.

June 29   Nothing worth putting down.

July 4, 5 & 6   People say the 'Itch' is in school. It is a lie, but many away in consequence. Have worked the children very hard.

The headmaster managed to acquire extra assistance:

School photographs in 1909 with Mr. Tipping as headmaster. Mr. Geo. Holdsworth, the visiting photographer, travelled extensively and his work can be found in many towns and villages

July 24   Mr. Tom Housecroft Student at York Training College is going to help me for the next 3 weeks.

July 27   Mr. Housecroft worked like a Turk both today and yesterday.

July 31   I hope to have another weeks work out of Mr Housecroft.

September 15   Caned a boy for swearing.

The Report of H.M. Inspector of Schools for 1865 noted that:

Considering that this school has not been a twelvemonth in operation, it gives promise of considerable efficiency. The younger children have been well taught, and with close attention to discipline and the teaching of Arithmetic especially the tables. I expect that by the next inspection it will be in excellent order. The present condition is very good for a commencement.

The headmaster, however, was not entirely happy with the progress of his pupils as the following entries show:

1866 February 23   Thrashed the stupidity out of J. Evans.

1870 June 1   Asked the first class
                    Who was Prime Minister of England. Got following answers:
                         1st The Pope
                         2nd Dr. Livingstone
                         3rd Archbishop Canterbury.
                    A boy writing a life of Samuel finished thus: 'when Samuel heard that the ark was taken he fell back and broke his neck, <u>and only the stump of him was left</u>'.

Nonetheless the school thrived.

1870 June 7   140 present this Morning by far the largest number ever in School at one time since I came here.

Pupil teachers were engaged at sixteen years of age, often from within the school, for a period of five years. Their salary was £8 per annum, increasing yearly. They were expected to study and their progress was monitored and examined annually with the inspection. A grant was paid to the school on their attainment of a satisfactory grade.

Although the work produced by the school appeared to satisfy the annual inspection, the conditions under which the children and teachers were working were far from comfortable, particularly in the bitter winter months but also occasionally in the summer:

1894 January 5   Fearfully cold today. Ink frozen in inkwells - only 104 children present.

Girls class c.1900 in the playground showing the chapel schoolroom in the background. This building was occasionally used as an overflow for school activities and visits of the school dentist

Infants class c.1910

1902 February 7   Very cold in school especially at the south end, where it is quite impossible to place any class for work, so that other portions of the room are crowded.

1902 December 3   A very dark day for the first time during the fifteen years of my work in this school I was obliged to light the gas in the forenoon.

1902 December 5   Bitterly cold day. In the south end of the room the thermometer at 10.30 registered 1 degree of frost.

1909 March 4   Thermometer only 2 degrees above freezing point. It is impossible to work properly in such a temperature.

1923 July 5   The children were very listless in school caused no doubt by the great heat. The infants took most of their lessons in the play ground under the elm tree.

The causes of absenteeism were numerous and show how important the children were at times of harvest in supplementing the work force:

1865 May 1   Several away engaged in barking the trees.

1865 July 10   Some away hay making.

1866 July 16   Attendance steadily increasing notwithstanding hay making time. I believe the parents take my advice and forgo the little gain they would get from the childrens labour, in order that they may attend school and make themselves better fit to cope with the world. Formerly there were parents who would keep their children out of school to earn 3d. Now they give up present gain for the boys' future good.

1866 September 17   Many children engaged in gleaning.

1867 September 17   Sent the pupil teacher round to enquire after the absentees. The general reason given was gleaning.

1867 October 14   Many children absent. Parents digging up potatoes.

1868 April 20   Barking began. This will cause a very thin school for many weeks.

1868 April 27   A very wet morning only 74 present many still working in the woods.

1868 May 1   Attendance poor and irregular.
Causes:- many gardening, potatoes being planted in the fields, and children engaged in the woods gathering bark. For which they earn 6-7shillings per week. Average attendance 93.

1868 September 16	Noticed several children away and on inquiry found they were going out in the fields picking acorns or 'mast' as they said.
1868 September 28	50 children absent this morning general reason given being 'after acorns'.
1868 October 26	Only 76 present. High wind Saturday night brought down the acorns: hence children are all after them this morning. One boy told me he picked 19 bushels which sold at 2s. a bushel. No wonder parents keep their children away.
1869 November 1	Very many away for various causes. Amongst others. Potato getting: gathering leaves to put under the pig.
November 2	Still more absent potatoes: cider: leaves.
November 3	More than 20 present today who were potato getting Monday & Tuesday.
1877 May 23	The barking season has taken away many scholars away for a time both old and young; for while the bigger boys are actually engaged in the work, the younger ones stop at home to keep house while their mothers go to work.
1886 July 2	Many away hay making.
1900 July 3	Hay making has considerably reduced the attendance this week.

In 1952 there was need for more room in the school and the assembly hall designed by the highly regarded county architect, Mr. Herbert Carr, was built. The wych elm, mentioned in the School Log Book, sadly had to go.

The huge wych elm, which once stood in the schoolyard.
Dr. J.D.K. Lloyd writes of it: 'A casualty during the building of the extension to the school was one of the finest trees in the district. This was a wych elm with an overall spread of about 100 feet and a girth of 15 ft 6ins at 5 feet from ground level. This tree, which stood where the assembly hall now is, was felled on 27th August 1952, when a count of its rings showed it to have been 179 years old. I gave this photograph of it to the school'

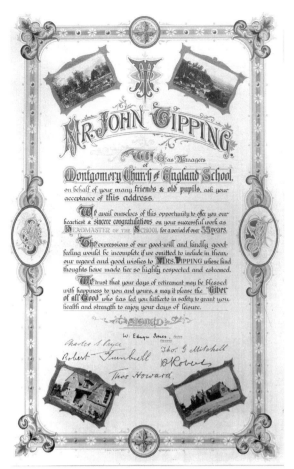

The illuminated address presented to Mr. Tipping on his retirement in 1923 following 36 years of service to the school

Recipe book for the cookery classes held in the Town Hall, 1894

Dairy Classes for young women in the Town Hall, c.1920

School photographs from the early 1930s

Towards the end of the nineteenth century there was beginning to be a general awareness of the benefits of education not only for children but also for adults. As mentioned elsewhere, the Calvinistic Methodist Sunday school introduced many poorer families to the pleasures of reading and writing. There were classes in the Town Hall for the women in, for example, cookery and dairying and the reading rooms originally in Princes Street and known as the Three Links Hall had a good lending library. Later, in 1924, the Institute given to the town by David Davies of Llandinam (see p.20) was aimed specifically towards education as well as relaxation and had a good reading room with newspapers and books.

Head teachers

1865-1866	Mr. J.D. Perkins
1867-1876	Mr. J. Jenkins
1976-1884	Mr. J. Moore
1884-1887	Mr. R. .A. Cuthbert
1887-1923	Mr. J. Tipping
1923-1952	Mr. M. Helme
1958-1961	Mr. E. Williams
1961-1973	Mr. W.E. Blair
1973-1995	Mr. M. Davies
1995-1996	Mr. H. Evans (acting)
1996-1998	Mrs. S. Hickey
1998-1999	Mr. C. Hamer (acting)
1999-	Mrs. B. Legge

7 Markets and Fairs

Following the granting of the early charters to Montgomery, markets were held each week on a Thursday. The burgesses were also allowed to hold two fairs each year, one at the

> 'ffeast' of St. Bartholomew, to continue for the space of four days, to wit, on the vigil, and day, and the two following days; and the other at the 'ffeast' of All Saints, to continue for the space of eight days, to wit, on the vigil and on the day of All Saints, and the six following days; and one Market there on Thursday in each week, with all liberties and free customs to such Fairs and Markets belonging.[1]

In the second half of the thirteenth century there was considerable agitation in Montgomery that the markets and fairs of Welshpool were to the damage of the King's markets and fairs at Montgomery.

> They say, that whereas the King has his market at Montgomery on Thursday each week, Gruffyd holds a market in his own town of Welshpool on the preceding Monday, at which market all saleable goods, which ought to be sold at Montgomery are sold on account of the nearness of the place etc.[2]

Following an inquisition of thirty-three jurors, damage was proven and the Welshpool markets were therefore moved to a site at 'Trefnant', probably that near Castle Caereinion, 4 miles from Welshpool. The political bickering rumbled on for some years, however, until Edward I held that the market and fairs in Welshpool had not been to the detriment of those at Montgomery, restored them and removed those at Trefnant. In addition, the number of fairs were increased to three, two of which coincided with those at Montgomery. The burgesses were not pleased. Much later, two extra fairs—on 15 March and 27 May and the days immediately preceding and following them—were granted to Montgomery by Charles II in his charter of 1670,

> as it would not be to the loss or prejudice of us, or any others, nor to the hurt of the neighbouring fairs.[3]

The May Fair is the only one that is still held, but does not correspond to any of the original ones. It takes place on the first Thursday in May and was probably connected with the medieval feast of the Translation of St. Nicholas, the patron saint, which fell on

9 May. Traditionally this was the day that servants and labourers were hired for the forthcoming year and it was originally known as the Annual Hiring and Pleasure Fair. These days Broad Street is filled with fairground attractions and families still come from far and wide.

The late Jim Pugh,[4] whose family farmed at Lymore for many years, talking in the early 1970s remembered that, as a young lad, the May Fair was 'one of the thrills' in Montgomery:

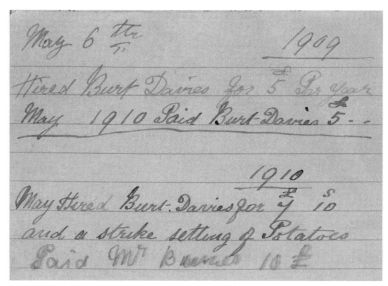

Entry in a notebook from the Old Castle Farm recording the hiring of Burt Davies for £5 per year in 1909. The following year he had a 50% pay rise!

May Fair in Broad Street in the 1920s. Pig carts are lined up on Church Bank in the background

Cattle on the left and pig carts lined up along Broad Street, pre-1920

We would love to see all the vehicles, horse drawn and steam engines on the main road to Montgomery May Fair. They used to unharness the horses from one vehicle and put two teams of horses onto another vehicle to take it up the hill.

Every farmworker was living near the work place in a tied cottage or farm cottage and practically every one of these had a pigsty to keep the pig. They would come to Montgomery May Fair. These pigs would be bought, they would be on the Church Bank in carts and they were what were called cart pigs. May time was the time to get these pigs out because a lot of the farm workers would only be paid once a year unless they wanted a shilling in the week perhaps, but actually they would get the full cheque at the end of the year and then re-hire again. They would go up the bank there and buy two pigs, so nearly all had bought the two if they had got enough money. So they would feed the two, [then, as they grew] sell [one] to buy the meal to feed the other. You would see them coming down with one under each arm carrying them home.

Mr. Bunner used to have bikes all out on the street for May Fair. He'd sell a terrific amount of pushbikes because that's the only time in the year that they would have a lot of money to spend.

Mattie Williams (née Bunner),[5] who lived at Burnt House, also vividly remembered her childhood visits to the fair:

There were hobbyhorses. They were all driven by steam in those days. There were shooting ranges and coconut shies. You could sit on a horse and go round and round

Busy market day crowds and cattle around Proctor's Shop in Arthur Street, pre-1920

Cattle being auctioned at the side of Proctor's shop, c.1905

The group of young Montgomeryshire farmers who formed a shearing party in 1931.
Back row L to R: Walter Humphreys, Sim Corfield (The Lack), Philip Davies (Stalloe), Jack Corfield (The Moat), Bert Howard (The Ditches), George Howard, Allan Bunner, Tom Mountford, Dick Davies (The Camp)
Front row L to R: Jim Bunner, Trevor Pugh, Ken Holloway, Bill Corfield (New House), George Mountford (The Pentre), Jim Pugh, Tom Price (Sutton)

Sheep auction in the 1930s. Mr. Ainge was the auctioneer and also to be seen in this picture are John Hamer, Emrys Breese, Maurice Jones, Malcolm Kinsey, and a young Frank Corfield

and round for a penny. They used to give us 6 pence each at home to go to the May Fair all day and yet we used to enjoy ourselves. They say they weren't making anything and yet they would go there. The old man with the oranges would throw them up in the air and give you a scramble for 'em you'd pay a penny each or something, the more you found the more you had and all that. It was very enjoyable.

Youngsters, nevertheless, were warned to beware of the temptations of the day, as in this extract from the *Corndon Magazine* of 1893:

A wet and muddy market day outside the Dragon, c.1910

Thursday May 4th is the day of the annual hiring and pleasure fair at Montgomery. Interested as we are in the welfare of all young people, we take this opportunity of affectionately warning them of the many temptations and snares, which will meet them on that day. Let it be by all means a day for innocent enjoyment and a pleasant reunion of friends and relations but it cannot really be a happy day if it is the occasion for excessive drinking which drags down the character and prepares the way for future misery. It is the power of everyone who prays for the Holy Spirit's help, to avoid that which is evil, and to refuse to go with companions who lead them into sin. A short and appropriate motto for each one would be those two words so oft repeated in Holy Scripture 'Be strong'.[6]

Market Day in front of the Old Bell in Arthur Street, c.1905. The notice fixed to the door post reads 'Hot Dinners 6d'.

During the 1800s, the livestock markets in Montgomery became increasingly popular and well attended and at the beginning of the twentieth century were thriving. They were held on the last Thursday

An impressive line up of beasts being shown Broad Street in the 1930s

in the month, and the February market in particular was regarded as the biggest and best in the county. Stalls with cattle and sheep, and carts full of pigs were set up on the cobbled pavements all around the town. Farmers used the same 'standing' each week and one can still find fixtures on some buildings to which were attached the gates and hurdles to pen the animals. The area behind the Town Hall was used as a sale ring. Following the sales the stock was driven down Pool Road to Montgomery Station to be taken by rail to its destination, unless it was bound locally. Jim Pugh recalled those days:

I've seen Broad Street that you couldn't walk down it—you couldn't move! Cattle used to be sold. I've seen 4 or 5 hundred cattle; there was only room in the yards to hold

Mr. Dick Jones, Llwynobin, and Arthur Morris with two prize winning beasts

*A proud line up of the award winning animals in the Baby Beef Show in Broad Street,
Autumn 1939*

perhaps not a hundred. The rest would have to stand on the streets and I've seen them
up Church Bank, again when they've been all the way up the Old Castle Road, very
near up the Old Castle top, all down Broad Street, all down Princes Street and Kerry
Street. You'd see them stood on either side of the road and poor old Mr. Maddox
outside his shop, we used to stand cattle there, and he'd come out every now and then
and wave his apron to stop them making a mess on the doorstep. It used to be a terrific
market. There were no lorries to take them away then, so they would all be driven
down to Montgomery Station in trucks unless they went locally.[7]

*Mr. Dick Jones with more cup winners outside the Dragon
at the May Fair, c.1939*

The considerable congestion in the streets and roads leading into the town in the early 1900s, led to the development of the Smithfield above and to the side of Rock House. The auctioneers were Morris Marshall and Poole, originally Morris and Cresswell of Chirbury, who also had branch offices in Bishop's Castle, Welshpool and Newtown. The increasing use of cattle trucks and decreasing use of the railway eventually sounded the death knell to stock markets in Montgomery. The last sale was held on a dank and dreary

The last cattle auction to be held in Montgomery, 1968

November day in 1968 after which the pens remained empty.

Interestingly, despite the loss of the stock markets, Thursday still remained the busiest day of the week in Montgomery, the farming community continuing to come to the bank to collect cash to pay their workers and do their weekly shopping. It has been very encouraging to see, over recent years, a slow but definite increase in the number and variety of market stalls continuing the tradition of trading in the Town Hall and along Broad Street.

The deserted Smithfield behind Rock House in the early 1970s

8   Trades and Professions

Immediately after Henry III's first visit to Montgomery, the building of the castle and, below it, the establishment of the town were under way and within four years, in 1227, the first royal charter was granted. Tradesmen and professional folk eagerly moved in and set up their businesses in the safe haven that the new settlement, protected by a wall and ditch, could now provide. In the early days of the town's existence the nature of many of the businesses was to supply and service the military garrison above the town, but as time went on and circumstances changed, the town developed the characteristics of a typical small country market town. Before the advent of modern transport, communities such as Montgomery supplied all the basic needs, not only of their inhabitants, but also of families living within reasonable walking distance. Farmers drove their stock to market and back within a day. Market days became an opportunity for country folk not only to sell their produce but also to visit the barber, order a dress or suit, get their clock repaired, have a new wheel fitted to their cart or visit the dentist and, of course, to socialise. Thursday was a particularly busy day for the innkeepers in Montgomery.

The Census returns for each decade from 1841 onwards list all the inhabitants of the town, street by street, with their ages and occupations. Trade Directories, which began even earlier, are also a valuable source of information, listing the different trades in the towns and villages within the area they cover. The earliest that has been found which includes Montgomery is *The Universal Trade Directory* of 1789, which, though rather sparse in its information, lists over twenty different trades in the town.[1] Later directories record a bewildering number of occupations in each street, often far more than there were buildings, and it is clear that many households provided several different services—particularly on market days. The Old Bell Inn, for example, offered, as well as meals and a bed for the night, a barber to shave the men and at the back a slaughterhouse and a washhouse. In addition the enormous bread oven would have been able to produce much more baking than the one household could consume. Other households provided a livery service. There were also many dressmakers and, as mentioned in chapter 6, several properties accommodated small private schools, often in an upstairs room and occasionally in the kitchen. There were at least four established clockmakers at various times in the town, but there were also quite a few residents who just did repairs. Similarly, in addition to the boot and shoemakers, many households offered a cobbling service. In the 1851 census there were over fifty entries with 'servant' given as the occupation, many of these accompanying the names of young girls who had been sent 'into service'. Their living quarters often left much to be desired.

Although the canal (1797) and eventually the railway (1862) passed quite some way from the town they were close enough to have an impact on the development of trades within the community. In *Pigot's Directory* of 1844, the entry for Montgomery reads:

> This Town was never signalised either as a place of manufacture or any great trade; but it has materially benefited since the opening of the Montgomeryshire Canal.

Carriers began transporting heavy loads from the canal wharf at Garthmyl over the River Severn to Montgomery. A sad event occurred in 1858, recorded by Samuel Lloyd in his notebook, which was found in the old tailors' workshop on the top floor of Chapel Place in the 1970s:

The notice on the centre of bridge at Caerhowel advises against this type of vehicle attempting the crossing! This steam roller, used on the roads around Montgomery for many years, was commandeered towards the end of World War II for work in restoring the roads in France but sadly the craft carrying it sank in the Channel where it still lies

> 1858, Jany 18. Carhowell bridg broke down under 2 wagons. Mr. Jones of Crankwell, Mr. Jones of dudson. 1 man kild on the spot Richard Grist he left a wife and three childrun.

Richard Grist was a carrier and had two cartloads of lime to move from Garthmyl to the two farms. The suspension bridge, which collapsed, was not approved of by the County Surveyor and had replaced a wooden bridge that was washed away in a flood in 1851. The present iron bridge dated 'Thomas Penson, Surveyor, 1858' rapidly took its place. However, there were soon concerns about its ability to support the weight of the

Montgomery station yard showing the Lion Hotel in the background and the newly made pedestrian access from the main road, c.1910

Montgomery Station with the yard and carriers, c.1890

newfangled traction engines. An iron notice, which can only be read on reaching the halfway point, warns 'persons in charge of tractors or other ponderous carriages against attempting the passage of the bridge'.

When the railway arrived, corn, coal, lime, slate and timber merchants set up businesses around the station and sidings and carriers provided transport for passengers and

Early photograph of Montgomery Station with staff and others, c.1890

Montgomery Station platform with train and passengers, c.1910

Horses were still being used for ploughing by some farmers locally up until the end of the 1930s

Owens hardware shop c.1920. Pen-y-grisiau was first altered by the addition of a new door and shop window and at the same time a petrol pump was installed on the pavement

luggage. The nearby Lion Hotel—'family, commercial and posting'—became a prosperous concern.

In 1895, with the horse still providing the main form of transport, Montgomery supported a horse dealer, two coachbuilders, four smiths, two saddlers and two wheelwrights. At the same time there were six grocers, four butchers, two bakers, five coal merchants, four tailors and four bootmakers—this for a population of a town that had shrunk from 1,286 in 1871, to 1,194 in 1881, 1,098 in 1891, and by slightly less to 1,034 in 1901, together with its hinterland. With the arrival of the motorcar, changes in the types of businesses began to occur. Those, which were horse related, started their decline, but probably less steeply in this agricultural community than in other, more urban areas. The roads began to improve and travelling became quicker and easier. Robert H. Bunner took over the ironmonger's business in Arthur Street from William Brown, and soon his other shop in Broad Street (Compton House) was selling bicycles and cars. Petroleum spirit was only available in two-gallon cans at first but eventually pumps were dispensing fuel both in Arthur Street and Bishop's Castle Street and still do.

R.H. Bunner is sitting on the right in the back of the car standing outside his shop in Broad Street (now Compton House) where he sold bicycles and cars, c.1910

Pen-y-grisiau in 1970. The Co-operative Association made further alterations in the 1930s by adding a further shop window

*The present garage at Rock House once housed
a thriving haberdashery business*

Later on, the County Garage, below the Cottage Inn on the road to Welshpool, sold petrol, serviced vehicles and provided a bus service. It was in operation for almost 30 years between 1960 and 1990. The increasing use of lorries specifically for moving stock was to cause the decline and final closure in 1968 of the cattle and sheep markets in Montgomery.

The number of active businesses today is very small compared with those thriving a hundred or so years ago. It is still possible, however, to recognise by the frontage of many houses where a shop or business had once been established. The addition of a bay window is nearly always evidence of an old shop front. In the early 1900s the large Georgian house known as Pen-y-grisiau (Tan-y-grisiau) in Bishop's Castle Street was converted into a iron-monger's shop, later becoming the Co-operative Stores with two large plate glass windows and a new entrance door, changes which would have made the Georgian designers turn in their graves. It was carefully restored to its original form in the 1980s.

*Charles Bryan Williams standing outside his
haberdashery and draper's business at Compton House*

The more important businesses were situated near to the Town Hall in Broad Street and Arthur Street. The present Spar shop has been a general grocer's for well over a century and was first established by Elizabeth James (wife of David, the tanner). William James and his sister Sarah were the next proprietors followed in succession by Robert Evans, Thomas Soley and Mr. & Mrs. Dick Roberts. Their daughter, Miss Margaret Roberts, was the last

CHAS. B WILLIAMS,
Broad-st., Montgomery,

BEGS TO ANNOUNCE THAT HIS ANNUAL

WINTER SALE

Will Commence Monday, February 19th, 1912,

And Continue for 21 Days.

C. B. W. wishes to state that he has purchased at a big discount a consignment
of Travellers' Samples, including a large quantity of

HOSIERY, PINAFORES, OVERALLS, HOLLAND & MUSLIN APRONS, &c., also

About 400 yards of Melton and Tweed Remnants,

Suitable Lengths for Ladies' Skirts, Children's Dresses and Boys' Suits.

These will be all MARKED at SPECIAL LOW and TEMPTING PRICES. He will also make Great
Reductions in Every Department, at such low prices so as to make a good Clearance for the coming season's
new goods. The Whole Stock will be carefully gone through and marked at such Tempting Prices that
must secure a quick Sale

The Items are to numerous to give full details, but below are a few Special Lines—

DRESS MELTONS, 6½d. per yard.
54-inch PLAIN AND CHECK HOMESPUN COSTUME TWEED, 1/7½ per yard.
PLAIN GREY UNION FLANNEL 3½d. STRIPED UNION FLANNELS, 5½d.
LADIES' LONG COATS from 7/11. GIRLS' PALETOTS from 3/11.

UMBRELLAS from 13½. SHIELD CORSETS from 13½d. (Very Special)

Ladies', Gentlemen's and Children's Mackintoshes

AT LOW PRICES.

MEN'S, YOUTHS' & BOYS' CLOTHING

IN GREAT VARIETY—

MEN'S SUITS	...	from 13/11	BOYS' SAILOR SUITS	from	1/9½
MEN'S OVERCOATS ...	„	10/11	BOYS' PALETOT SUITS	„	2/11
YOUTHS' OVERCOATS	„	4/11	BOYS' NORFOLK	„	3/11
BOYS' REEFERS	„	2/11	YOUTHS' TWEED	„	8/11
BOYS' TWEED KNICKERS	„	10½d.	MEN'S CLOTH VESTS	„	1/11½

And a large lot of Odd Garments will be marked very Cheap to clear.

☞ Yorkshire BLANKETS from 4/11; White Blankets from 2/11½; Blanket Rugs
from 1/11½ each. These are some *very* Special Bargains.

REMNANTS AND BLOUSE LENGTHS—A Large and Varied Lot.

CALL AND SEE SOME REAL GENUINE BARGAINS.

TERMS: CASH.

Phillips & Son, Printers, Newtown.

C.B. Williams sale poster 1912

*Thomas Alders the first recipient of the old
age pension in Montgomery, standing
outside the post office on the corner of
Kerry Street below the Dragon, 1909*

Chemist shop and post office

private owner. Across the road, Compton
House, the present Post Office, was C.B.
Williams draper's shop after R.H. Bunner
removed all his business to its present site in
Arthur Street. The two shop fronts are still
identical. The Post Office has changed its
location over the years—for two separate
periods it was in the Old Bell, in 1874 it was
being run by William Marshall in conjunc-
tion with a chemist's shop at the house now
called Braemar, and later next door in the
house below the Dragon now known as the
Grosvenor. There are records of two other

Thomas Lucas outside his painting and deco-
rating business in Broad Street, c.1911.
The roof of the house was raised at a later date

chemists. F.J. Nash from Newtown had a branch in Princes Street, and around the same time in 1924 Rowlands of Wrexham opened a branch at Tan y Castell in Broad Street when they rented the shop from the Lucas family who were plumbers and glaziers. The Gornall family ran a similar business further along the street, and in the house in between dwelt Valentine Ashton, a horse breaker and dealer and his family.

Next door to Compton House, the present HSBC Bank is the latest name in a series of banks to occupy the building, the first of which was the North & South Wales Bank in the nineteenth century. At the other end of Broad Street, the Nat West Bank is a relative newcomer, being estab-

In 1924 Rowlands the chemists of Wrexham
opened a branch in a room rented from the
Lucas family

*North and South Wales Bank established
in the late 19th century*

lished in the mid 1920s as the National Provincial. The bank named the property Cullen House. On the same side of the street there are two adjoining houses, which were not given the Georgian facelifts that all the neighbouring buildings received in the late 1800s. Castle Kitchen was previously a grocer's shop (most recently Jellings). The late Miss Edith Powell clearly remembered attending a private school there. Next door, Country Works Gallery, until quite recently known as either the Nurse's House or Oak Cottage, was once a public house called The Oak, although there is some disagreement about which of the two old buildings housed the inn.

Across the road, the corner shop, now a florist, was once Purslow's, a gentleman's outfitters and before that Albert Williams, greengrocer and confectioner. There are records of a school once occupying an upstairs room. Further along Broad Street, the long established Checkers Hotel with the adjacent butcher's shop were run together for many years by E.T. Davies, father and son successively. There was a slaughter house and 'clem

*An early photograph of Broad Street showing James grocer's shop and beyond the Checkers,
Parlow, the clockmaker*

Albert Williams, fruiterer and confectioner, on the corner of Broad Street and Princes Street, c.1920

house', a building where the animals were starved for twenty-four hours prior to killing, in the yard at the rear of the Checker's together with quite extensive stabling (E.T. Davies Snr. bred horses for trotting races). This whole area has recently been converted to office accommodation and renamed Princes Square.

Arthur Street is particularly interesting. The row of half-timbered houses between the Town Hall and the garden opposite Bunner's is thought to be a 'market incursion'—an area originally used for temporary market stalls which over the centuries gradually became permanent. Businesses were conducted

Gornalls, painters, plumbers and decorators established their business in Broad Street in 1901. The first and second floor windows above the two doorways on Gornalls are both painted, either having been filled in as a result of the Window Tax, or representing the need for Georgian symmetry

from all the buildings in the row. David Proctor, probably the earliest professional photographer in the town, had a general store on the end nearest the Town Hall. In the early 1970s, following a change of ownership, a fine collection of his glass plates was discovered in the attic, many of which have been used in this book. Next door is the Old Bell, now a museum but a hundred years ago a Temperance Hotel, which at one time, as well as offering the services mentioned above, sold toys and newspapers. The date when the premises were last licensed is uncertain. Next door was Joseph Burroughs the clockmaker and next door to him, another member of the Proctor family, Dick, who was a boot and

E.T. Davies and his butcher's van in Chirbury with Johnny Spittletree, whose real name was John Davies. He was an odd job man who lived at Myrtle Cottage and had once been a wheelwright, hence his nickname, (the spittletree is the large wooden hub of the wheel)

E.T. Davies with his delivery van outside the Checkers Hotel and his butcher's business, 1920s

David Proctor's shop in Arthur Street showing a part of the market area to its left

Burroughs, clock and watchmaker next to the Old Bell in Arthur Street

Dick Proctor on the steps of his boot and shoe shop in Arthur Street

shoemaker as was his father, William, before him. At some time prior to 1700 the two end dwellings were a public house known as the Plume of Feathers, and were bought, restored and let by the council in the 1960s to provide some of the earliest-built council accommodation in the country.

Opposite David Proctor's shop, the second house down was for many generations a solicitors' office, Williams, Gittins & Tomley being the last occupants. Charles Sidney Pryce, William Wilding and Edmund Edye, all of whom had held the post of Town Clerk, practised from these premises. Behind the site of the present Institute was William Jones' wheelwright's and blacksmith's shop. His name is inscribed on the hubs of the secondhand fire appliance that the council bought in 1893. The large square brick building further down the street was built by the Williams-Wynn family of Meifod as a hotel variously known as the Wynnstay Arms or the Cross Foxes. Next door, R.H. Bunner & Son Ltd. has been established in the town for more than a century. Robert Bunner bought the business from William Brown whose family had been ironmongers and blacksmiths for many years. Mr. Brown was a great supporter of royalty and was responsible for building Alexandria Terrace in Chirbury Road and Victoria Buildings in Duck Lane, which he renamed Princess Street. It has since lost an 's' and is known today as Princes Street.

The large dwelling below Bunner's is the White House, the home of medical practitioners for nearly two

The half timbered houses at the lower end of the row in Arthur Street were at one time the Plume of Feathers

hundred years. Richard Baxter, Surgeon, who was also the medical officer for the Workhouse, almost certainly lived there in the late 1700s and he was followed by George Towns, Surgeon. Two brothers, Dr. Henry and Dr. Robert Cockerton, who also kept hounds, practised from there around 1870. Dr. Thomas Morgan was there in 1889 and he was succeeded by Dr. Dick Kirk. In 1924, having just lost his wife and in failing health, Dr. Kirk employed a young doctor from Northern Ireland as a locum, initially for two weeks. Dr. Kirk's health failed to improve and Dr. Samuel James (Jim) Stewart continued to run the practice. He was a hard worker and very soon was able to buy the practice from Dr. Kirk. He married Doris, a daughter of J.E. Tomley, the solicitor, and was the last doctor to live in the White House. He retired in 1963 but continued living there until his death. The successful medical practice that he had established eventually became a partnership

Dr. Thomas Morgan who ran his medical practice from the White House in the late 1800s

of four and moved from Arthur Street to its new custom-built premises in Well Street in 1982.

Following the closure of the Gaol in 1878 most of the building was demolished leaving the octagonal governor's residence, which served as a home for a series of doctors. Dr. James J. Robertson and Dr. Reynolds lived and worked from there in the early years of the twentieth century and after the First World War, the notorious Dr. Game Phillips set up in practice there. Both he and his wife were over-fond of drink, and older residents could remember him firing his shotgun at imaginary assailants late at night. He eventually became bankrupt and when the bailiffs came, nearly all the furniture was taken, leaving the couple with just the kitchen table. He promptly arranged for the legs to be sawn off so that he and his wife were able to sit on the floor to take their meals. Despite his eccentric behaviour, he enjoyed a good reputation, but this may have been due to his policy of making the diagnosis in most patients attending with chest complaints, serious or other-wise, of bronchial pneumonia—in those days a seriously life-threatening illness.

Dr. Abbot, for a short time, had a small practice in Alexandria Terrace and Dr. James Powell Wilding held his surgeries in Kerry Street. Dr. Nicholas Watson Fairles worked for a brief period only in Broad Street. After marrying the wealthy Miss Mercedes Humphreys he became Nicholas Fairles Humphreys. He moved to Bank House, became much involved in local politics and never practised again.

A blacksmith's shop adjoined the stone house (now called Steppe House), across the street from the White House. Harry Pennie and his son Glyn were the last to work there. Harry's father Edward had taken over the business from Thomas Bridgewater. Further

William Hamer showing one of his newly made poultry houses

Charlie Statham, seen on the right outside his workshop, with his men sawing planks from a huge oak trunk

John Powell tailor and grocer with some of his family outside his shop in Chapel Place

along the bank, William Hamer, who lived in Princes Street, and his son Silas had a joinery business. The somewhat ramshackle buildings below Hamer's were more recently Arthur Baldwin's carpentry workshop where Charlie Statham, the last undertaker to live in Montgomery, once carried out his trade. Chapel Place, the brick terrace next to the Wesleyan Chapel was built for the Powell family who came from Chirbury in the 1870s by a relative, Samuel Lloyd of Princes Street. John Powell and his family lived in the bottom house where they kept a grocer's shop and ran a tailoring business.

The old stone walled pound, at the crossroads, where stray animals were held until their owner paid the fine for their release, was replaced shortly after the Second World War by a memorial garden. In the early 1900s two old women, one of whom was affectionately known as 'Auntie Polly' lived in a single storey, slate-roofed, stone building on the site and looked after the public mangle and weighbridge. A public house known as the Plough stood at one end of the terrace of houses known as Plough Bank overlooking the pound. It was from there that one boarded the Rea Valley Engineer, the coach to

Newtown that ran every Tuesday, Friday and Saturday, and to Shrewsbury every Monday, Thursday and Saturday. At the Chirbury Road end of Cross Houses a bake house was run by a Mr. Williams whose son was nick-named 'Harry the Bake house'. J. Eaton and later P.R. Eaton had a butcher's shop at the foot of the steep School Bank. This was, at one time, called Muffin Lane because a Mrs. Bishop who lived at Whitecroft sold excellent muffins.

Cross houses, c.1910

The Pound showing the weighbridge with Whitecroft and the Baptist Chapel in the background. Driving past in their pony and trap are Mr. and Mrs. Dick Roberts, who ran the grocer's shop in Broad Street, c.1920

Down Chirbury Road there were as many as seven families selling milk at one time and numerous small shops selling a variety of goods. The row of houses called Clive Terrace is also known as Factory Bank. This name is somewhat of a mystery as no one has been able to establish what was manufactured there. Further down the road on the site of the present Fire Station stood The Montgomery Gas Works. Electricity was comparatively late arriving in the town and the gas works provided power for domestic use and street lighting for some sixty years from 1857. In 1888, the owner, Dr. Fairles Humphreys sold the business to Thomas Mourby who was manager until 1922. Mr. Mourby was a former Chief Engineer in the Merchant Navy, who had been running gasworks in Rhayader and Builth. In the early 1900s he was Captain of the Montgomery Fire

J. Eaton and later P.R. Eaton ran the butcher's shop below Whitecroft at the foot of School Bank. Here John Eaton is seen with his traditional Christmas Show in 1888

MONTGOMERY.

CHRISTMAS SHOW.—Mr. John Eaton's show of Christmas cheer consisted of two splendid maiden heifers, fed by the Ex-Mayor W. Jones, Esq., six Welsh wether sheep, fed by Mr. Owen, Jamesford, two by Mr. W. Rogers, Bacheldre Hall, and some nice porkers by Mr. Hamer, Montgomery. The premises were neatly decorated on Friday and presented a very attractive appearance.

J. Eaton's Christmas Show, 25 December 1888, as described in the local newspaper

Brigade. Opposite the gas works there was a builder's yard associated with The Brades. These semi-detached houses next to Alexandria Terrace were built and lived in by the Jones' family. Arthur Jones had a grocer's shop in the first, and John and Maurice Jones and more recently Reg Jones lived next door and were builders and coal merchants. Reg Jones was a well-known figure in many organisations within the town and a prominent member of the Town Council. He was elected an Honorary Freeman in 1951.

Princes Street, a very steep thoroughfare, much narrower than Arthur Street, was the main route through the town and, from newspaper reports, the scene of numerous accidents involving horse drawn vehicles. Many of the Princes Street businesses over successive generations revolved around the leather industry. Lewis Griffiths had a saddler's business at the top end of the street next to the Checker's yard and there were harness-makers and boot and shoemakers. Up until relatively recently the late Harold Davies was making hedging mittens at the back of his shoe shop next door to the Buck Hotel. There is a strong tradition of pleaching in the border counties of Wales and the tough and long-lasting mittens were and still are in great demand throughout this area. Norman Davies, his son, still carries on this craft.

In Bishop's Castle Street, as mentioned earlier, Owen's ironmongers changed the face of Pen-y-grisiau, to be followed by the Co-op, which closed in the mid 1970s. Next door, the motorcar business was originally owned by Bob Lloyd and across the road Hurdley House was the home of Sydney Winkup, a Veterinary Surgeon in the first half of the twentieth century. Winkup was preceded by a Scotsman, James McGavin, who lived in a house, demolished in the 1960s, opposite Bunner's shop. The site of the old tanyard is in Back Lane round the corner from the Crown Inn. In Kerry Street there were yet more small shops, Williams' bakery and the Gullet public house.

Mr. Croft and Harold Davies outside their respective businesses in Princes Street, c.1920

Harold Davies in his workshop making hedging mitts

Today Montgomery boasts six public houses, quite a number for a small population of just over 1,000: the Dragon, the Checkers, the Crown, the Cottage Inn, the Bricklayers Arms and the Lion down at Caerhowel. In 1650 there were no fewer than sixteen inns and alehouses licensed, as seen in the following item presented to the Grand Jury of the Great Sessions held at Welshpool dated 8 April 1650:

> Wee present the number of twenty and four Innes to be licenced within ye toune and liberties of Poole and no more,
> ... the number of sixteene Innes and ale houses in ye toune of Mountgomery to be likewise licenced.[2]

W. Tanner, painter and decorator, with his motorbike and sidecar outside Burdett Row, Bishop's Castle Street

The Dragon Hotel behind the Town Hall is perhaps the oldest and certainly the most important of all the hostelries. Sometimes referred to as the Green Dragon it is an old coaching inn with a long history. Owned by Lord Powis, the first recorded landlord was Richard Jones in 1770 when the rent was £26 per year. It was from here that one boarded The Dart, the coach from Kidderminster to Aberystwyth 'on Mondays and Fridays in the bathing season at 12'. There are records of inquests being held there and many important properties changed hands at auction sales. Traditionally the local hunt met in front of the hotel and it was the centre of activity on market days.

Early references to the Dragon in topographical publications were not always complimentary as in this description by John Byng in *The Torrington Diaries - A Tour to North Wales 1784*:

... when we reentered our inn, (Green Dragon, Montgomery; only wants cleanliness) and sat down to look at supper; for we selldom eat any. Here began a specimen of Welsh dirt; for my blankets stunk so intolerably that I was oblig'd to use a quarter of a pint of brandy to sweeten them.

Conditions improved, however, and *Slater's Directory* of 1868 has the following entry:

The principal Inns are the Green Dragon, the Wynnstay Arms and the Checkers, all of which, visitors will find very commodious.

The Buck Hotel in Princes Street, shortly after it had closed in 1968

And in 1874, *Worrall's Directory* states encouragingly that:

> The principal hotels are the Wynnstay Arms, the Checkers and the Dragon, at either of which the visitor will find every comfort and attention.

The Checkers in Broad Street has always played an important role in the social life of the town with its large function room at the rear used for dances and wedding receptions and traditionally has been the venue for the annual cricket and football club dinners. The Bricklayers Arms once known as the Masons Arms, is mentioned in the account of the Coming of Age celebrations of Lord Clive in 1839 when a sheep roasting and dinner took place. The Crown and the Cottage Inn have long been established but little of interest has been found about their past history.

Among the hostelries which no longer exist are The Buck Hotel, (now T'yr Carw), in Princes Street, which closed in 1968. Old photographs show large buildings to the rear, which contained the malt house and brewery (see p.16). One of these served as a meetinghouse for the Calvinistic Methodists in the early days of the movement.

The Bow and Arrow, also called the Plough and Harrow, (now Rock House) lay behind the Town Hall and was closed in about 1785. Its associated malthouse, however, functioned until 1839. There is a bill from Jake (?John) Griffiths to the Earl of Powis for thatching the Plough and Harrow (and also the Falcon, see below) in 1771-2 among the Powis Estate records.

The half-timbered Gullet in Kerry Street was demolished in the 1930s, a new pair of brick houses being built on the site by the council in 1938.

The Wynnstay Arms in Arthur Street with its spacious ballroom was reputed to have been bought and licensed by the Wynns of Wynnstay for electioneering purposes, as the Herberts held all the other public houses in Montgomery in which to 'regale' their supporters. This story is unlikely to be true, however, as no particular Herbert v. Wynn election contest ever took place. It was sometimes known as the Cross Foxes, as seen on the Wynn Family coat of arms.

The Plume of Feathers was in the pair of timber-framed houses almost opposite the Wynnstay and was closed prior to 1700. The houses are mentioned in an early eighteenth century deed as 'formerly the P. of F.'

The Oak (now Country Works Gallery) in Broad Street was also known as The Falcon between 1784-1900. It was re-thatched at the same time as the Plough and Harrow in 1771. It was said to have had 'a ballroom', but it is difficult to visualise where this could have been as the rooms are so very tiny that little dancing could have taken place.

The Piggin Tavern below the castle rock was sometimes called the Pig and Whistle. It is not known when it ceased to be licensed, for it was only remembered as being a small shop by John Davies, the sexton, as a child in the 1860s:

> They used to sell lovely apples and they also baked large currant cakes which they sold by the slice to passing carters. There was wagons passing all day and every day nearly with wood, lime etc.[3]

Little is also known about the Horse and Jockey (now the Ramparts) on the Kerry Road. The Plough overlooking the Pound was functioning at least as late as 1868 as the following entries in the School Log Book show:

| 1868 21 September | Many children away picking acorns and home with the Cider Mill at the Plough: whom I must talk to tomorrow |
| 23 September | Punished two children for staying away to see the cider making yesterday. |

Much cider was made locally. The cider press was transported from farm to farm, on all of which were apple orchards for cider making. As many as 850 gallons of cider were made on a farm for consumption by the workers, as can be seen from the bills from Mr. G.H. Bunner, the owner of the press.

Many of the licensed properties brewed their own beer, and many households did likewise. As Mattie Williams recalled:

> We always had home brewed beer at the table for dinner and we never had such a thing as cups of tea, a jug of home brewed beer and none of us drunk you know. Of course me Dad drank enough to sail to America.[4]

Other people remember otherwise:

To be a teetotaller was one of the pillars of the teaching in both our chapel [Presbyterian] and the Wesleyans. Have you noticed the number of public houses in Montgomery with a population of under a thousand? Drinking to excess was a problem in the town as I suppose it was countrywide. The Wesleyans and Presbyterians had the evils of drink as one of their main planks (Mary Reed).[5]

Concern regarding the evils of drink resulted in the formation of the Band of Hope.
Many children were persuaded to sign the pledge at an early age.
However, the temperance movement was not universally supported!

9   R.H. Bunner & Son Ltd.

Robert Henry Bunner was born in Marton, Shropshire on 2 October 1872. His parents were John and Mary Bunner who lived at the Manor House and ran a four hundred acre farm. The 1871 Census records that they employed eight farm servants and two domestic servants. Whilst still a very small child, Harry, as he was then known, lost his father who was thrown from his horse in the snow and froze to death. He was sent away to school in Newtown aged only seven or eight years of age. On reaching fourteen and leaving school he expected to receive a legacy of around £2,000 from his late father, but due to either mismanagement or possible embezzlement this money had disappeared. From 30 April 1887 he became apprenticed for four years to Mr. Arthur Greenhous, an ironmonger in Bishop's Castle, when he was paid £10 per annum.

Meanwhile, his mother had remarried a John Statham and produced two more sons, one of whom, Charles, became a carpenter and undertaker in Montgomery. It is likely that she came to live in the town after her second marriage.

In 1891, Mr. Samuel Brown's long established ironmonger's business in Arthur Street came on the market. This was about the time when 'Harry' Bunner's apprenticeship in Bishop's Castle was coming to an end. At the age of only eighteen or nineteen he must have shown great determination and considerable persuasive powers to

Robert Henry Bunner as a young man

111

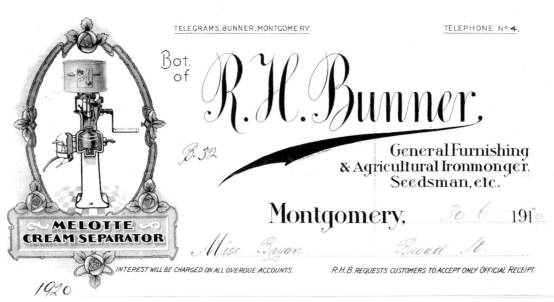

R.H. Bunner's billhead in 1920

Early photograph of Bunner's Arthur Street Shop, c.1905

This is possibly the first tractor sold by Bunner's ploughing at Jamesford Farm just outside Montgomery

find a backer prepared to advance the loan of £600 needed to purchase the business. Robert H, Bunner, General & Furnishing Ironmonger, Seedsman, was founded.

Young as he was, he rapidly gained a reputation as a shrewd and effective businessman. He stood no nonsense and was something of a martinet, his staff holding him in considerable awe. His entrepreneurial activities were legendary, it is said that shortly before the First World War, he bought a thousand ploughs, causing major congestion at Montgomery Station. At another time he effectively cornered the nation's supply of binder twine having read in the papers of an impending shortage! He soon expanded the ironmongers and furniture business to deal in agricultural machinery and as early as 1903 he established a Massey agency. His other shop in Broad Street, now the Post Office, sold Raleigh bicycles and by 1920 was selling and hiring motorcars. At one time all the Austin cars sold in Wales came through R.H. Bunner's.

Perhaps the most famous of all his ventures was the development and popularising of the Montgomeryshire Late Flowering Red Clover. He actually discovered the seed in Scotland, brought it down to Wales and took it to Aberystwyth University where it was given

Bunner's staff with three combine harvesters, c.1950

the local name. The seed was packed in sacks each weighing two hundredweight, and two of the strongest men in town, Ned Evans from Chirbury Road and Charlie Lloyd from Sarkley, were always employed to carry them up the ladder into the seed store. It was sold all over England, Wales and Scotland for decades until its decline in popularity in the 1950s.

R.H. Bunner became a well-respected member of the community and a prominent churchman. In 1902 he married Annie Smith Allan, of Scottish ancestry, and they had four daughters and a son. Annie died tragically as a result of an accident on Christmas Day 1935 and he died in 1947, leaving the house and business to his son Allan and daughter-in-law Mary, with generous legacies to the four girls. The name of the firm had become R.H. Bunner & Son in 1939 and remains that to the present day. Sadly, Allan Bunner died at a relatively young age in 1953 leaving his wife, who had two young daughters Anne and Mary, to continue running the business. With the assistance of loyal staff and the wholehearted support of the local farming community, Bunner's survived a difficult time.

'Old Man Bunner', as R.H. became known, would appear to have passed on to subsequent generations the ability to look ahead and gauge the markets. Changes in farming practices have gradually modified the business. Mrs. Mary Bunner recalls three combine-harvesters being delivered all at the same time with the problem of where to put them, but now the firm no longer deals with large agricultural machinery. These days quad bikes, lawnmowers and other small machines are sold and serviced. Stoves, cooking equipment and fancy goods, as well as all the usual ironmongers items are available. A large percentage of the income now comes from the tourist trade, for visitors enjoy the personal attention and old world ambience Bunner's continue to provide. The family tradition continues, today two of R.H. Bunner's granddaughters and a great-grandson work for the firm. Rob like his grandfather, Allan before him, is a fine bowler and a regular member of the Montgomery Cricket team.

10   The Tanyard

The complex of buildings and pits which comprised the long established tanyard, was situated at the junction of Back Lane and Bishop's Castle Street behind Burdett Row. Nothing remains of them now. An entry in the parish registers dated 30 October 1603 reads 'Maria, filia Johannis Lloyd, coriarii [tanner]'. The will of Jenkin ap Rees of Montgomery, dated 1628 mentions a 'tanhouse thereto belonging, in the tenure of Reignald Lloyd'.[1] The Lloyd family continued to run the tanyard from that date for a further two hundred years into the first quarter of the nineteenth century when, in 1816, David James, having learnt the trade of currier and tanner in Llanfair Caereinion, took over its management. His son, Edward Rees James, succeeded him.

The tanyard not only provided employment for the tanners but also for those engaged in collecting bark, an essential ingredient in the tanning process. The numerous oak trees, found in the neighbouring Lymore Estate, provided a plentiful supply of bark. They were felled by the men in the spring and the womenfolk stripped the bark using metal rods with a spoon like end, known as 'barking irons', whilst the children collected the strips and stacked them in the carts. This resulted in frequent absenteeism from school during the 'barking season' in April and May, as has already been seen in entries in the early school logbooks on p.77. Others include:

1868 April 20	Barking began - this will cause a very thin school for many weeks
1868 May 1	Attendance poor and irregular. Causes - many gardening, potatoes being planted in the fields, and children engaged in the woods gathering bark for which they earn 5 to 7 shillings per week.
1877 May 23	The barking season has taken many scholars away for a time both old and young; for while the bigger boys are actually engaged in the work the younger ones stop at home to keep house while their mothers go to work.

The oak bark was stacked in a tall stone building with the front open to the roof, which would contain up to 80 - 100 tons of bark at a price of about £4 a ton. Stacked in the summer, it stood till the next year when the strips were ground into small pieces by a horse-driven mill, ready for use in the tan pits. These, about twenty in number, were housed in a long covered shed and were fed by a stream which ran through the yard and out into the Nant-y-celyn brook. The hides were first soaked in a pit containing a weak mixture of oak bark and water, and were lifted out and turned three or four times a day. They were then gradually transferred to other pits with stronger and stronger mixtures with less frequent lifting. The whole process took about a year to complete depending on the thickness of the skin. Another ingredient in the early stages of the tanning process was dog faeces. These contain enzymes which help to soften the hides allowing the tannins

Building used for storing the oak bark to the right alongside Back Lane with the leather-dressing shed to the left

*The old drying shed; note the louvered windows at the top.
(The round-headed windows were later additions)*

from the oak bark to penetrate. The amount used required great skill and experience and apparently the dog's diet greatly influenced the effectiveness of its waste product, a diet mainly of animal bones producing the best material. Dog fouling would have been a rare problem as this product was carefully collected and commanded a good price from the tanner.

The tan pits were considered to be good for curing the skin diseases of animals and one head tanner, Mr. Fletcher, could be persuaded

The leather dressing shed

Back Lane showing the old tanyard buildings on the right

to dip dogs brought to him 'when in a good mood' it was said. He would also allow children to purchase two pennyworth of 'dubbin' (a mixture of oil and tallow used to dress leather) for shoes or to take a small supply of tan 'to back up the fire'.[2]

The drying shed was a two-storey building with adjustable shuttered windows in the upper storey. The round-headed windows were later insertions. A further shed was used for dressing the hides. Reuben Maddox (1859-1947) employed by Mr. Edward Rees James, recalled the dressing being carried out on a mahogany table about ten or twelve feet long. In those days, when a shoemaker had an order for new boots he would go directly to the tannery to select a suitable hide.

The tanyard closed in 1893 and the buildings were used for housing timber and cattle, and finally as a garage for the repair of bicycles and cars. The site was sold to the Town Council for the erection of the old peoples' bungalows in Well Street, and all the buildings were demolished in 1966.

11   Clock and Watchmakers[1]

From the middle of the eighteenth century the long case clock, often referred to as the grandfather clock, was becoming a fashionable piece of furniture, spreading to the homes of those other than the wealthy and leading to a profusion of clock makers throughout Wales. These long case clocks had a painted, enamelled or brass dial, and some were highly ornate. The case was usually made of oak by a carpenter, often the local undertaker, but later could be obtained from specialist suppliers. Each area had its own favourite style of case. The oak was sometimes coloured to imitate the fashionable mahogany, and inlays of more expensive woods were popular.

It is not known how far the early Montgomery clock makers manufactured their own mechanisms, but in the second half of the nineteenth century the practice had grown almost universally within Wales of importing the movements and faces from clock making centres, with the clockmaker's name inscribed or painted on the dial. The cases may well have continued to be made locally. Four Montgomery watch and clock-makers are to be found in the trade directories. The earliest record was of George Williams of Broad Street (1835). There is a very fine engraved watch in a silver case, hall marked 1832, now in the National Museum of Wales, of which the movement, verge (the earliest type of escapement, controlling the power) and fuseé (a device for evening the time-keeping for the length of the winding—probably one week) were all made by Williams. The cock is of finely engraved and

Finely engraved watch in a silver case dated 1832 made by George Williams of Broad Street. By kind permission of the National Museum of Wales

119

pierced work, with a mask. The dial is of brass and engraved in the centre with an enamelled chapter ring and an outer border engraved:

KEEP ME CLEAN AND USE ME
WELL
AND I TO YOU THE TRUTH WILL
TELL

Later directories record William Mills in Church Street (1844 *Pigot*), Alfred Parlow in Arthur Street (see p.97) (1868 *Slater*) and Broad Street (1874-1887 *Worrall*) and Joseph Burroughs in Arthur Street (see p.100) (1889 *Suttons*, 1895 *Slater*).

At the turn of the nineteenth century the clock maker gradually became a clock repairer only. Interestingly. many old clock plates are inscribed with the signatures of the repairer together with a date, the practice of the time. The following names have been found on clocks in Montgomery:

A.J. Giles	Nov. 1908
	June 1911
W. Palmer	24 March 24 1909
	18 May 1929
	18 Dec. 1930
	(three different
	clocks)
Mansell	24 April 1918
(never used	
his initials)	
Joseph	
Burroughs	21 Feb. 1898
Alfred Parlow	No date

Face of a long case clock made by George Williams in 1826

Face of a long case clock made by William Mills, Church Street (Church Bank)

12   The Gaol

Military garrisons have always provided secure facilities for the housing of prisoners and in Montgomery, the Norman motte and bailey castle and the later stone castle were no exceptions. The first record of a prisoner, a certain Hywel ap Rhys, can be found in the *Chronicle of the Princes* dated 1115,

> That Hywel had been in the prison of Arnulf fitz Roger, Earl of Baldwyns Castle, to whom King William had given a portion of Rhys ap Tewdwr. And at last that Hywel had escaped from prison in a maimed state after his members had been cut.[1]

The unfortunate Hywel would have been confined in Roger de Montgomery's castle built at Hen Domen.

Later, Henry III's castle overlooking the new town of Montgomery was described in a survey of 1593:

> The said Castell of Mountgomery ys Scituatt one a Rock wch gathereth in ye Toppe small, The Castell being builte as the Sictuacon requireth somewhat long sowth and northe.
>
> In primis, at the entring into the Castell there ys a gate howse sowthward wth two small closse Roomes therin underneth for prisoners as seameth ...[2]

No records survive of the prisoners who occupied these dismal cells.

Following the demolition of the castle in 1649 there is further reference to a gaol in Montgomery in the account of 'That Ancient Servant of the Lord, Richard Davies', the Quaker from Welshpool:

> About the third month, 1660, many of those Professors, Captains, Lieutenants & Soldiers, that were in Arms in Oliver's and Richard Cromwell's Days were put in Prison in the Town of Montgomery.[3]

The site of this prison is not known.

Up until the early nineteenth century, prison was not a form of punishment as such but usually a holding place for people before trial or, if convicted, awaiting their fate—corporal punishment, transportation, or execution. Less serious offenders were punished by confinement and humiliation in the stocks or the ducking stool. The old town stocks were moved to the Museum of Welsh Life at St. Fagan's in 1951 after being stored in the bottom of the Town Hall for many years (see p.169). It is not known when and where they were last erected for the purposes of punishment, but it was most probably outside the Town Hall. Montgomery's ducking stool used to punish scolding women was sufficiently

unusual, in that the miscreant was ducked in the standing position, to warrant the following description by Blount:

> Whereas through Scolds and Whores many Evils arise in the Town, viz. Strifes, Fightings, Defamations, &c. and many other Disturbances by their Shouting and Bawling, our Practice concerning them, is, that when they are taken they are adjudged to the 'Goging Stoole' and there to stand with their Feet naked, and their Hair hanging down and dishevelled for such Time as they may be seen by all Persons passing that Way, according to the Will of our Chief Bailiffs.[4]

The punishment was possibly carried out at the lower end of Princes Street (once known as Duck Lane). Prior to the building of the Baptist chapel (demolished in 1966) at the bottom of School Bank, the site was occupied by an open cesspool.

The first building to house the County Gaol still exists and is sited on the left, half way up the steep, narrow road known as the 'Conduit' (locally pronounced Cundit), leading up to the castle behind the Town Hall. The local Justices built it in about 1735 to serve the county, and it was originally more extensive than the surviving row of three residences now called Castle Terrace. The gaoler received a small salary

The first county gaol built c.1735 now a row of houses known as Castle Terrace

that he was entitled to enhance by collecting fees from the inmates. His house, for which he paid rent, was immediately opposite the prison on the other side of the track, but few traces of it now remain.

In a survey of the County Gaol at Montgomery dated 26 March 1774, Thomas Pritchard found the building to be far from satisfactory and reported, among other problems:

> The two dungeons, which are small rooms only, eight feet by seven, have the floor quite rotten on account of the water gushing through the back wall under the timbers. There is no ceiling only a naked floor over them, which is very unsafe. The back walls are extremely damp and unwholesome by reason of the earth lying against them.[5]

The famous reformer, John Howard, visited the gaol in 1788 and also published an unfavourable report[6] on what he found there. His words were evidently heeded, for in the report to the Justices by Mr. Nield, a well-known philanthropist, following his visit in 1803, it was noted that conditions had somewhat improved:

> This gaol is finely situated, on a rising ground. Here is one courtyard for men and woman debtors, 44 feet by 32 with a sewer in it; a day room, 14 feet square, and a small room adjoining it, fitted up with a bath and boiler. Above stairs they have also 8 good sized rooms, three of which are free wards. The County allows no bedding, except straw on the floor. The keeper furnishes beds at 1s. 6d. per week the single bed, but 2s. per week if two sleep together. The men felons have a small courtyard, and a day room, with six sleeping cells on the ground floor, the average size being about 8 ft. 6 inches by 7 ft. and 9 ft. 6 inches high. Also, upstairs, two sleeping rooms or cells. The women felons have likewise a small courtyard; a day room, with one sleeping cell on the ground floor, and two bedrooms above stairs; to all which the County allows wooden bedsteads, with straw, two blankets and a rug. A large room, over the entrance door of the Gaol, is used as a chapel, but not partitioned off so as to keep the classes - male and female, distinct from each other. A small room is set apart for the sick, but the well was out of repair, and no water accessible.

Mr. Nield also included in his report a short review of the staff and inmates:

> Gaoler, John Davies; salary £35, Fees, debtors 8s 4d., besides which the under-sheriff demands 7s 6d. for his liberate [fee paid by the prisoner for his release at the end of his sentence]! Felons pay no fees. For conveyance of transports, one shilling per mile. Garnish abolished [this was the fee extorted from a new prisoner by the gaoler]. Chaplain Rev. Charles Williams, salary £20, duty, every Sunday prayers and sermon, and visits every day those who are under sentence of death. Surgeon, Mr. Jones, for felons only, salary £8. Number of prisoners, Sep. 8, 1803: - Debtors 3, felons, &c., 10, lunaticks 3 ... Allowance, sixpence a day each, in bread.

There follows a description of the three 'lunaticks', of whom the third:

> Aaron Bywater, kept walking quickly about, backwards and forwards, as far as his chain tether would permit; but there was something in his eyes so highly ferocious, that, being alone, I did not like to speak to him, or come within the length of his tether ...[7]

In 1805 the gaoler's account of this unfortunate man, who is thought to have been a member of a well-to-do family in Kerry, noted that:

> He is a lusty young man of the age of 35 years: was committed to this gaol in 1799 charged with the wilful murder of Jacob Stanley ... he was kept constantly ironed and chained down in this gaol till the beginning of 1800, when having his handcuffs off one day for the purpose of exercise ... he ... barbarously murdered a convict ...; since which time it has been deemed proper ... to keep him in close confinement, which must naturally gradually impair his constitution and ultimately terminate his existence ...[8]

Thomas Edye, a Solicitor and Town Clerk for many years, writing in *Bye-gones* in 1878 said that he had a clear recollection of 'the circumstance [of the murder in the gaol] although only ten years old at the time':

> The murdered man was not a convict, but a debtor named I believe, Salisbury Davies, who being about to be released, on the evening before the day he expected his discharge, was chopping some wood for the purpose of cooking a supper which he intended to treat the unfortunates he would leave behind. On stooping down to place the wood in a position for the purpose, Bywater snatched up the axe and clove the poor fellows skull. The then Lord Hereford, who resided at Nantcribba, and Mr. Herbert, of Dolforgan, near Kerry, and of which parish Bywater was a native, met together as magistrates the next day at Montgomery, and I was among the audience on their investigation of the case, and it was then as a matter of course Bywater was transferred to the criminal side and tethered as Mr. Nield describes him to have been. Ultimately he was sent to Old Bedlam and then transferred to New Bedlam where he died about 15 years ago, having probably reached the age of 90 or thereabouts.[9]

Bethlem Royal Hospital Archives reveal that he actually died in 1848, at the age of 85, having been incarcerated there for thirty-two years. The case of Aaron Bywater produced much contemporary concern regarding the inadequacies of the system in providing appropriate care for 'the lunatick' whilst protecting the public.

The Gaol Order Book for Montgomery Gaol (1804-1837) makes interesting reading and sheds light on the conditions that prisoners had to endure. During the early 1800s the welfare of the prisoners was increasingly cared for in respect to their bedding, clothing and certain modest comforts. Prison inmates could:

FELON ESCAPED.

BROKE out of Montgomery Gaol, in the night of Friday the 30th of October, 1795, EDWARD BARRAT, convicted of Burglary, and under Sentence of Transportation. The said Edward Barrat is a Native of Forden, in the said County of Montgomery, about 60 years of age, a very short man, not above five feet high, humpbacked, round shouldered, and very broad across he breast, bald headed, with grey eyes, and light hair, inclined to curl, and pale complexioned. Had with him when he went away, a brown coat, a blue and white striped linsey upper waistcoat, and a red under waistcoat, and a pair of pocket fustian breeches. He has travelled great part of North Wales, Shropshire, and Cheshire, as a Pedlar.

If any person will apprehend him, and lodge him in safe custody, he shall, on giving information, receive TWO GUINEAS Reward, besides what is allowed by Act of Parliament, from me

WILLIAM DAVIS, Gaoler.

Felon escaped - notice in the Salopian Journal *of 5 and 11 November 1795*

send into the town for provisions and necessaries by the gaoler's servant every day at the hours of Seven, Ten, and Twelve in the forenoon, and at Three, Five and Eight in the afternoon, and at no other time, and that these times be signified by ring of the bell.[10]

In 1816 an Act of Parliament abolished the taking of fees from prisoners. The entry for 31 June 1818 recorded that the annual salary of John Davies, the gaoler, had been consequently advanced to £78 for the gaol and £20 for the House of Correction, with effect from the Epiphany Quarter Session of 1816. Out of this sum, the gaoler had to pay the turnkey's annual salary of £18.

At about the same time as the first County Gaol was built, a building which probably served as a simple 'lockup' was in use at the lower part of the town. Somewhat confusingly, it was described both as the 'House of Correction' and the 'Bridewell' by different authors. Standing at the corner of Pool Road and Gaol Road it is now known as Manor House and Nos. 1 & 2 Black Hall Cottages. Its purpose was the confinement of criminals of either sex who misbehaved

The old house of correction in Pool Road

or had been sentenced to hard labour. The dank, overgrown underground cell has been identified, by measurement, as that described in John Howard's *The State of the Prisons*, 1792, and Mr. Nield's report in 1803.

Montgomery House of Correction, - Keeper, H. Lloyd; salary £12 13s. 4d.; fees 2s. 6d. Garnish, not yet abolished, is one shilling. Surgeon, if wanted, is sent from the town. Prisoners, Sep. 8, 1803, two. Allowance, 4d. a day, in bread.

Remarks.- There is only one courtyard for all description of prisoner; with a dungeon 13ft. by 9ft 3in., to which the descent is by nine steps, and within it a whipping

Mont Q/AG 3/3

Names	Age	Crime	When and where Tried	Orig.l & present Sentence	Character as far as known	State of Health
Mary Hughes	28	Felony	Pool Spring G.t Sess.n 1818	Transported 7 years	Not Known	Healthy
John Powell	26	d.o	Pool Spring G.t Sess.n 1819	Condemned Reprieved on Condition of being Transp.d Fourteen Years	d.o	d.o
David Jones	20	Horse stealing	d.o	d.o	d.o	d.o
John Rogers	25	House breaking	d.o	d.o	d.o	d.o
Samuel Hill and John Fletcher	28 24	Forgery	d.o	Transported 14 years	d.o	Sam.l Hill Not Healthy J. Fletcher Healthy

John Davies gaoler

A document listing the convicts under sentence of transportation in the gaol on 23 July 1819.
By kind permission of Powys Archives

post. On the ground-floor are two middle sized rooms with four wooden bedsteads, and loose straw. Seven persons at a time had been confined in the dungeon, and as many also in the two rooms. The employment of the prisoners is spinning.[11]

With the creation of county constabularies during the mid nineteenth century, Manor House achieved the more dignified status of Montgomery Police Station, and the stone building within the rear angle was built to extend the accommodation. Here had formerly been the prisoners' exercise yard, and the original abutments of the immensely high stone wall which enclosed it may still be seen on the back corners of the two wings. The constabulary moved to the more modern premises in Chirbury Road in 1937.

Although there are reports of capital punishment being carried out in Montgomery, these are far fewer than one might have anticipated when no less than 200 different felonies could lead to the scaffold. Where possible the death sentence was commuted to transportation to the

Montgomeryshire Great Session.

EXECUTION —On Monday last, William Tibbot, a native of Llanllwchaiarn, capitally convicted at the Great Session held last week at Welsh Pool, for the murder of his own father, John Tibbot, was executed at Montgomery. It appeared that the deceased was proprietor of the house occupied jointly by the prisoner and himself; that in consequence of the son not paying the rent due to the father, the latter caused a distrain to be made, and afterwards served an ejectment on the prisoner, who, in consequence, avowed an intention of murdering his father, which threat he put in execution by causing poison to be administered to him. The wretched man, prior to his execution, confessed the crime of which he had been found guilty, as also that he murdered his first wife in a similar manner.

[We purpose giving the trial of William Tibbott in detail in our next Journal.]

At the same Great Session, judgment of death was recorded against *Robert Poppet*, for stealing a mare, value £15, the property of Edward Pearce, of Churchstoke ; and against *Joseph Swinley*, for stealing a sheep, the property of John Clayton, of Llanmerewig.—*Edward Lewis*, for breaking into and robbing the dwelling house of Edward Davies, of the parish of Manafon, was sentenced to be transported for life.—*Edward Goodwin*, the accomplice of Joseph Swinley, in stealing a sheep at Llanmerewig, was sentenced to be transported for 14 years.—*John Butler*, for robbing the dwelling house of Francis Steel, of the Bellan, in the perish of Pool, was sentenced to be transported.

1830 report in the Salopian Journal *of the execution of William Tibbott, the last person to be hanged in Montgomery*

Interior of Montgomery Gaol, c.1870

colonies. The condemned cell had become 'the ante-room to either the New World or the Next'.

The place of the last executions was probably just below the old Gaol and above the Town Hall but the house known as Crogbren (Welsh for gallows) may well have been an earlier site of a more permanent scaffold or gibbet. The last person to be hanged in public in Montgomery was not, as is sometimes thought, the celebrated 'Robber', John Davies who was hanged in 1821 (see also pp.32-33), but a labourer called William Tibbot who had murdered both his wife and his father. A detailed and somewhat gruesome account of his trial and subsequent execution appears in the *Salopian Journal*s of 18 and 25 August 1830.[12]

In the early 1820s attitudes regarding the treatment of offenders were hardening and pressure from central government steadily increased in favour of total convict separation from the general public. The distinction between gaol and house of correction had already disappeared in all but name: labour for all was to be, in the official wording, 'of the hardest and most servile kind in which drudgery is chiefly required'.

Clearly, the old county prison on Castle Hill was falling out of date and beyond conversion. In 1827 land for a new gaol was bought from Lord Powis at the northern end of the town. In 1830 Montgomery New County Gaol began to rise from the ground, to a design of the architect Thomas Penson of Oswestry, later to become County Surveyor, whose plans, based on a Home Office standard, largely reflected the new policy of total separation.

The only description to be found of the new building is in Samuel Lewis's *A Topographical Dictionary of Wales* dated 1833:

> The County Gaol and House of Correction at the lower end of town, on the left of the road to Shrewsbury, was built at an expense of £10,000, defrayed by the County. It is a handsome edifice of stone of a durable quality, procured from the rock on which the castle stood, and is arranged in the form of a cross, having the Governors house in the centre, the whole being enclosed within a boundary wall upwards of 20ft. high. The Governor's house commands a view of all the wards, and of the working of the tread-

mill which is a double one, having a wheel in the felon's yard and the other in the vagrant's yard, and the machinery being so contrived, that the labour can be regulated according to the force supplied. The building comprises six wards, with spacious airing yards to each, in two of which are a tread wheel and an engine house to provide the prison with water. Above the engine house and tread wheel is an infirmary, with two sick wards and Matron's rooms, and over the Governor's apartments is the chapel, to which there is a separate entrance from each ward, beyond the chapel is a ante-room leading to a committee room for the visiting Magistrates, and two waiting rooms, and on the roof, over the entrance and turnkeys lodge is a place of execution.[13]

1832 was a busy year for John Davies, the gaoler up on Castle Hill, as the new building at the lower end of town neared completion. On 1 November he records altering the beds 'so as to make as many of them as may be fit for the New Gaol'; while on 6 December he is instructed to order coal 'for airing the New Gaol'. At last, on 7 December the male prisoners were removed to the new institution. The females were to be detained in the House of Correction, which had been suitably renovated, 'until the female appartments at the New Gaol are completed'.[14] By the end of 1836 the women's ward at the New Gaol was apparently ready to receive them. At any rate John Davies' Order Book finally closes with a simple shopping list dated 12 January 1837, and he then goes into retirement as tenant of some grazing land belonging to Powis Castle. His only memorials are entry number 47 in the Castle Rent Book for 1836, and his tombstone in the churchyard (see p.33).

Darkness descended upon the prisons. The local community was increasingly excluded, and it is significant that from this time on it becomes ever harder to discover what went on behind the gaol gates.

The original entrance to the New Gaol was from Chirbury Road, adjacent to the site where Plas Offa was later built. The brick-built coach house nearby housed the governor's coach and horses. Later, access was made from Pool Road, which was at first just used by prison traffic such as

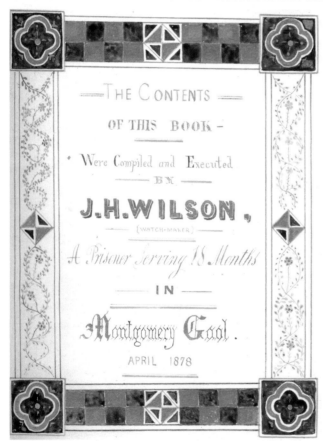

The front page of an illuminated book of poems written and illustrated by J.H. Wilson, whilst a prisoner serving eighteen months in Montgomery Gaol just prior to its closure in 1878

View of gaol in the early 1970s showing the surviving cellblock wall (now demolished) to the left of the octagonal governor's residence

the Black Maria and wagons carrying stones from the quarry nearby for the prisoners to break. This became Gaol Road, and led to the late addition of the imposing classical gatehouse portico dated 1866 built to the design of the architect J.H. Poundley of Kerry, a one-time pupil of Thomas Penson.

The first act of nationalisation was to put an end to many small county gaols. By an Act of 1877 the ownership of all local prisons passed without compensation into the hands of the Secretary of

The imposing Gatehouse was added in 1866 with the new access along Gaol Road

State at the Home Office, who valued Montgomery Gaol at £2,409 12s. and required the property to be put on the market. On 1 April 1878, in common with many other local prisons throughout the country, the gaol was formally closed, all prisoners having been transferred to the national prison at Shrewsbury.

Mr. Mytton, a Welshpool wine merchant, bought the property for the much reduced sum of £1,450 and

Cellblock wall, 1978

soon much of it was demolished, the dressed stone being widely distributed in the neighbourhood. A major purchaser was Mr. William Gwalchmai James who built the nearby

Cell window, 1978

house to be known as Plas Offa. Its stone gateposts and those of the Presbyterian Chapel both originated from entrances to the prison. All that now exists are the remains of one cellblock wall and the Governor's residence. This has been occupied over the years by successive doctors, the Civil Defence, various squatters, a toy factory and most recently housing association flats, while the other original staff dwellings remain in occupation, two of them in the resplendent gatehouse.

13 Fire Service

Every community is threatened by the destructive potential of fire. The closely built houses in the ancient Borough of Montgomery in past centuries were mostly thatched and timber-framed and greatly at risk. There must have been provision for tackling fires but little recorded knowledge exists of the arrangements in the early years. Prior to the insurance companies' involvement, each local community had their own informal procedures. The following reminiscence suggests that even relatively recently the communal human bucket chain arrangement was being used to tackle fires within the town.

> In the 1890s there was a chimney fire at Hurdley House - very dangerous because the beams of the original malt house went from wall to wall through the chimney breasts (These of course were built up when the building was converted into a dwelling). Everybody left work to help (or just to watch). Mr. Gornall sent all his men with ladders, and a human chain was formed; Will Cuckoo went up on the roof. Buckets were passed up to him, and as he didn't know which flue was alight, he poured water down all of them to make sure. Next day there was a little cleaning up to be done in six rooms. Each side of the chimney breasts were fitted cupboards, so as the brick wall was hot there was a danger of the cupboards smouldering. So all that night men were stationed in each room with a bucket of water and a cup to splash water over the wood. Will Cuckoo was one of these.[1]

Fire mark of the Salop Fire Office at one time on the old Forden Workhouse

The first organised fire brigades were those established by the Fire Insurance Offices, starting in London but quickly spreading to the rest of the country. To identify the properties for which they were responsible, each insurer fitted a firemark to the outside of the buildings they insured, and the Salop firemark started appearing prominently on buildings in the Montgomery area following the formation of the Salop Fire Office in 1780. Its own fire brigade was maintained in Shrewsbury, and it was expected to travel as far afield as Montgomery. In those days of slow transport, one wonders how many fires had burned themselves out well before the brigade reached the scene.

The arrival in Montgomery in March 1893 of the secondhand manual fire engine changed everything. The borough council had purchased it from the Alliance Fire Office in Shrewsbury, which had absorbed the Salop Fire Office in 1890. This appliance, manufactured by one John Bristow of Ratcliffe Highway, became that of the Montgomery Borough Fire Brigade. The instructions for the machine's use, were displayed in a glass-fronted frame mounted on the front boarding of the driver's seat, and are printed below:

DIRECTIONS

By JOHN BRISTOW, of Ratcliff-Highway

ENGINE - MAKER

For keeping the largest Size Engines with
Suction in Order, viz:-

When the Engine is hard to Work, pull up the Board, which hath my name on it, also lift up the little Board at the Bottom, by the Staples, and Oil the insides of the Barrels when the Forces are down; Oil the Chains, and both ends of the Spindle or Pevets; and if the Chains become slack, take the fork Key, and screw up the square Nut on top of the Forces, till they are tight. When needful take off the Carriage Wheels, Grease the Axle-tree Ends. When it hath play'd very much dirty Water, play clear Water, that the Engine May be cleans'd. Grease the Elbow with Tallow, and do not screw them too hard on, neither screw them off, but screw the Branch off only, because the Leather Pipe, when used, screws on to that Place; Then the Branch is to bescrewed on to the other End of the Pipe or Pipes, for the Screws fit each other. When the Pipes are not likely to be used for some time, let all the Water drain out; and after they are dry, coil them up, and hang them in a dry Place: Before they are used again, Liquor them with Neats-Foot-Oyl and Tallow, at least once a Year. Some Men may work the Engine with their Hands, and others with their Feet; but take a full Stroke from the Top to the Bottom: When you use it to Water Gardens, fix the Fan to the End of the Branch, and the Water will diffuse itself like Gentle Showers.

When it is play'd be Suction, screw off the Cap that hands by a Chain, and screw the Sucking-Pipes on the same place, and turn the Handle above, from the Letter A to B. When it plays out of the Cistern only, turn the Handle to A again, let some Water be in.

If the Forces in Time wear loose in the Barrels, they may easily be taken out, by screwing off the Nut at the Top, and another at the Bottom. This will free both Ends of the Chain from the Forces: With a Key like a T unscrew two Pins, that hold the other Chains in the Iron-wheel, which will give Liberty to draw out the Threadles. With the Fork-Key unscrew two Nuts, lift the Spindle out of its Place and draw it back, then the Forces may be taken out, and beat broader with a Hammer, and the Leathers screwed up harder, and more Leather added [indecipherable word]: Afterward put the Forces into the Barrels again, and screw all together as before - Paint the inside of the cistern once in Two Years in Order to preserve it.

Captain Thomas Mourby with the old fire pump behind the town hall, c.1905

The first page of the newly formed Montgomery Fire Brigade minute book, 1894

Eight volunteer firemen were to be enrolled by the town council and were paid a retaining fee of 5s. per year, plus 2s. 6d. for each of four drills to be performed during the year. The first seven firemen were appointed by the council on 25 January 1894, and comprised Thos. H. George, Maurice Davies, J.E. Tomley, Henry Jones (Church Bank), John Davies (Church Bank), Reuben Maddox and Alfred Eaton.[2]

In the report of the first fire attended by the newly formed brigade, its captain drew a number of concerns to the attention of the town council:

Fire upon premises occupied by Mrs. Bridgewater in Arthur Street, Montgomery.
22nd September 1894.

Capt. T.H. George, Firemen R. Maddox, A. Eaton, J.E. Tomley, H. Jones, M. Davies present.

Gentlemen - I beg to report that at 2 o'clock on Saturday morning a fire was reported to me to have broken out on premises occupied by Mrs. Bridgewater in Arthur Street. The Fire Engine was got out and used until 4 a.m. and the services of the Brigade (of whom 6 were present) were required until 5 a.m. when they were discharged the fire having been thoroughly got under. The chief efforts of the Brigade were taken up in preventing the fire spreading beyond the building in which it originated and this I am pleased to say was satisfactorily accomplished. The fire having got so thorough a hold upon the smithy before we were called, it was utterly impossible to arrest its progress there. Beside the Brigade there was a crowd of willing helpers but great difficulty was experienced in the matter of water supply, the engine often and again having to be stopped on this account. I cannot however feel that I have as yet responsible charge of the Brigade and its appliances, no rules or regulations having been framed or specified for their management. I should be glad to have the instructions of the Council as to the payment of the Brigade and the Engine charges. Neither the premises destroyed or their contents were insured but I do not doubt the insurance company will pay its share on account of the proximity of the adjoining property on which insurances have been taken out, further as to upon whom is to devolve the keeping of the accounts and memoranda connected therewith. Also in case of a call to places at a distance I should be glad to know to what limit we are restricted and what arrangements are made for horsing the engine. The keeping of the key or duplicate keys of the Engine house is also an important matter, the hall-keeper, in whose charge the only keys now existing are resides at the opposite end of the town and this added to the difficulty of getting the engine from its awkward resting place is productive of dangerous delays. Clothes and equipment for the members of the Brigade are urgently needed, also 5 more jointing keys.

Thos. H. George
27th September 1894

Thomas George's pleas took a long while to be dealt with if the rules laid down 40 years later are anything to go by:

Montgomery Fire Brigade

RULES and REGULATIONS drawn up by the Town Council at a Meeting held on
30th June 1932
----

1. The Fire Brigade shall be called the Montgomery Fire Brigade and shall consist of:-
   8 members (Including the Captain and Vice Captain)
   2 reserves

2. All appointments to the Brigade shall be made by the Town Council and shall be subject to notice on either side to be given at least two days before any Council Meeting to expire on the date of the next Council Meeting.

3. ALL Members of the Brigade shall be resident in the Town (i.e. within the Lighting Area) and on ceasing to reside within that area shall automatically cease to be members of the Brigade.

4. ANY member of the Brigade on reaching the age of 55 years shall retire automatically but the Council may extend such members service until the age of 65.

5. THE Fire Engine, Hose, Uniforms and all other appliances or Gear are the property of the Town Council.

6. THE Fire Brigade shall themselves appoint a Secretary (any age limit not to apply in this case).

7. THE Captain shall have the entire management of the Brigade when its services are required at a fire or at a practice; in his absence the Vice Captain as next in superiority will be considered the officer in charge.

8. There shall be four practices held each year. On convenient dates to be fixed by the Captain as follows:-

   2 'Wet' Practices
   * 2 Hydrant Drills

   All members shall attend all practices unless prevented by illness or with permission of absence given by the Captain.
   * NOTE These Drills to be fixed only after consultations with the Borough Water Engineer and if there is surplus water available.
   The Captain shall report after each Practice or Drill on the condition of the Hydrants or any repairs required.

9. EACH member attending Practices shall be entitled to be paid FIVE SHILLINGS for each practice

10. THE Captain shall detail the members of the Brigade in rotation for cleaning the Engine and other appliances after Practices and each member so detailed shall be paid FIVE SHILLINGS.

11. THE Brigade shall be responsible for keeping the Engine and other appliances clean and in proper working order and also attend the proper drying of Hoses etc., after Fires or Practices.
   The Captain shall report immediately to the Town Council any defect in the Engine or apparatus.
   Each member shall be responsible for the Uniform, accoutrements and other appliances served out to him and keep each uniform clean and in repair.

12. THE Brigade if required to do so shall attend all official Functions of the Town particularly the Mayors Sunday Parade.

13. THE charges for attendance at Fires shall be as follows:-

Use of Engine	£3 3s. (except to the Alliance Assurance Company)
Captain	15s. for 1st hour and 1s. 6d. for each subsequent hour
Vice Captain	10s. for 1st hour and 1s. 3d. for each subsequent hour
Firemen	10s. for 1st three hours and 1s. for each subsequent hour

The Captain if he considers necessary may appoint Official Helpers at a Fire and he shall certify any such helpers and keep a record of hours worked.

14. EACH member on joining the Brigade shall subscribe his name to these rules, in a book kept for the purpose, in proof of his willingness to submit to all such rules and regulations and also such alterations as may subsequently be made by the Town Council.

Each member will receive a copy of all such rules and regulations.

The engine was, of course, horse drawn to fires, but whenever horses were not readily available on drill nights, it was customary to affix tow-ropes to the pump and pull it by hand to the drill point at Lymore Pool, about three-quarters of a mile away. As the route to the pool was downhill from its station behind the railings at the back of the Town Hall, it was necessary, on such occasions, to solicit the goodwill of members of the public in assisting to drag the pump up the hill back from the drill. It is understood that this procedure continued, even sometimes in the case of actual fires, as late as 1938.

From the earliest days of the brigade, Montgomery firemen were uniformed, but it was the policy not to replace a uniform whenever there was a change of personnel, and any new recruit had to take over the uniform of his predecessor whether it fitted or not! The Captain was always appointed by the council, but whenever a vacancy arose in the position of Vice Captain it was the usual custom to fill this post by placing the names of all the serving firemen in a hat, and drawing one out. The Captain and his Vice Captain were authorised to engage the temporary services of 'helpers' at fires at a rate of 1s. per hour. The record of one such fire indicates over seventy helpers having been engaged, the assistance being as 'pumpers' on the manual pump.

The town council agreed that fire cover should be provided beyond its boundaries and should extend to the districts of Kerry, Llandyssil and Chirbury. Mutual assistance arrangements were eventually arrived at with the nearby fire brigades of Newtown and Welshpool. For many years there had been particularly keen rivalry between the local brigade and that of Welshpool. Many incidents occurred at fires attended by both

Fire practice by the Nant-y-celyn Brook outlet near Burdett House, c.1905

The Fire Brigade with the old fire pump behind the town hall, c.1905

N.P. VAUGHAN PRYCE,
SOLICITOR,
TOWN CLERK.
Telephone No 3.
J.E.TOMLEY,
SOLICITOR,
CLERK TO THE JUSTICES.
Telephone No 8.

Town Clerk's Office,
Montgomery.

Fire Brigade. Scale of
Pay for Fires. —

Captain — 15/= for first hour
1/6 an hour afterwards
Vice Captain — 10/- for first hour
1/3 an hour afterwards
Firemen — 10/= for first 3 hours
1/= an hour afterwards
Helpers — 1/= an hour.

Original Rules approved
in June 1895

brigades in the rural area between the two towns, until the agreement was reached that the first Captain to arrive would be accepted by all as the one in charge of handling the incident.

The old manual engine remained in use up to 1939. The council, however, feeling that some modernisation was desirable, latterly fitted a tow bar to enable Reg Jones' coal lorry to take the place of horses; a great deal of precious time could be lost in catching horses which were out to grass on a dark night. The very first occasion for the new motive power to go into action was in response to a fire near the Blue Bell Inn. All went splendidly until, when rounding a bend at high speed within sight of the fire, the old iron wheels and axles became so overheated that one wheel seized up. Fortunately for all concerned it was a Saturday night. All the firemen having been drinking freely in the local pubs, and not lacking a talent for improvisation, they quickly found a means of cooling the overheated wheel hub, which thereupon was freed, thus enabling them to proceed to the fire.

In passing, one must acknowledge the standard of workmanship that went into those early appliances. The Deputy Chief Fire Officer for Denbighshire and Montgomeryshire Joint Fire Service, the late Mr. D. Wheway-Davies said in 1965:

Document enclosed in the Fire Brigade minute book showing the scale of pay to firemen for attending fires in the 1930s

> When I last saw the engine it was still in working order and its condition was a real credit to the man who manufactured it some 70 or more years previously.[3]

In 1941 the old manual pump was supposedly moved from Montgomery to a Cardiff Museum. This was not however the case. After a long search, prior to the town's charter celebrations in 1977, it was traced to the Mid Glamorgan Fire Service Headquarters at Lanelay Hall in Pont y Clun, having been carefully restored.

By 1939 the borough council had joined with the neighbouring councils of Forden, Welshpool and Llanfyllin to form the North Montgomery Joint Fire Board. Under this joint agreement Montgomery retained its own proud identity and its own command, but now enjoyed the acquisition of a Beresford Stork light trailer pump under the Auxiliary Fire Service wartime scheme. During the war Montgomery continued to function as a 'one pump retained station' of the National Fire Service, the only major change being the issue to the station of a whole-time towing appliance.

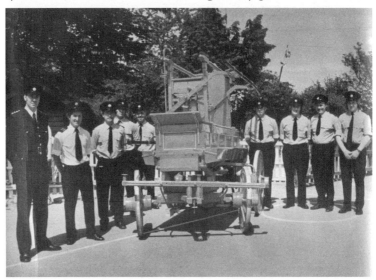

The restored old fire pump on display in the school playground during the 1977 charter celebrations

The coming of the Joint Fire Service, covering the areas of Denbighshire and Montgomeryshire, in place of the N.F.S. in 1948, brought little or no material change to the Montgomery unit, which still retained its 'one pump retained' status. The pump and equipment continued to be housed at the rear of the Town Hall, whilst the towing vehicle was garaged in a corrugated iron shed some distance away. Neither provided any pretence of staff accommodation, and it is to the great credit of the local personnel

Pre-war photograph of firemen behind the town hall.
L to R: Albert Weaver, Ruscoe, Rowlands,
Fred Weaver, Jack Bishop, Ernie Weaver

The crew of the Fire Brigade in 1960 in front of the newly opened station in Chirbury Road.
L to R: Geoff Morrall, Jack Tanner, Tom Weaver, John Blower, Sid Lloyd, John Burd, Nick Davies, Fred Weaver

The Fire Brigade in front of the Water Tender, Bedford T.K. in May 1988.
Back row, L to R: Philip Haycock, Richard Howells, Norman Davies, Chief Fire Officer Stan Horner, Brian Evans, Geoff Andrew, Leading Fireman Ambrose Williams.
Front row, L to R: Leading Fireman John Burd, Ray Bishop, Phillip Evans, Sub-Officer Glyn Morgan, Eifion Lewis, Dave Lea

that keen interest in the service was maintained in spite of such lack of facilities.

In 1960 the Joint Fire Service built a brand new Fire Station on the present site on Chirbury Road, where the town gas works once stood. The new station provided all that could be desired, and soon a modern appliance was in operation. Thus, nearly seventy years after its formation, the fire brigade in Montgomery was at last provided with facilities that enabled the unit to maintain a standard of fire cover equal to that applying to any other comparable area in the country.

Serving in the Fire Service has frequently been a family tradition in Montgomery. Albert, Ernie and Fred Weaver were three of a family of eleven children brought up at Crogbren who became part-time firemen. Shortly before his death in 2001 at the age of ninety-nine, Fred recounted his memories of the old manual pump:

The pump was kept at the back of the Town Hall where the toilets now are, behind railings with a gate, which was locked. There was a box with a glass front set in the wall with a key in it. In the event of a fire, the glass was broken, the key the key removed, the gates opened and the bell [now in the Town Hall] was rung to summon the brigade. In later years, volunteers were called by a siren on the Town Hall.

The brigade consisted of eight firemen. The pump was worked with six men each side standing on a platform, all volunteers, mostly farmhands as most of the fires were on farms. It was quite hard work pumping. It was possible to shoot the water over Forden Hospital. There were a lot of fumes associated with the hay fires. The firemen had to cut the stack down the middle to let the fumes out. The firemen were engaged mainly in moving the hay. When all was over the Captain organised the pay for the volunteers, giving them a slip of paper to present to get their money.

One had to apply for a vacancy. It wasn't difficult to get. Pryce Davies, the rabbit catcher who was almost blind was engaged. The firemen were all older, none young. I was the driver of Reg Jones' coal lorry when the wheel went on fire. The fire was at the 'Three Jacks' by Mellington Lodge. Horses were kept up the Kerry Road by Bevan, the cobbler from Tafarndy. An Austin van was used for towing and was kept in a corrugated shed at the Checkers.

Fred Weaver was getting on for seventy years old himself when he retired from the brigade.

14   Sports and Pastimes

The area where Roger de Montgomery built his castle was situated in the Domesday hundred of *Witentreu*. This was immediately east of Chirbury to which manor the hundred was attached and is now known as Whittery. In 1066 it was described as being waste, and held by three Saxon thanes—Sewar, Oslac and Azor—as a hunting ground. Deer and wild boar would have been their prey. Over the centuries, the thrill of the chase has continued to excite many country dwellers. Hunting became formally organised in the 1800s and at least three different hunts—the United, the Tanatside and the David Davies Hunts—are

Alderman and Mrs. C.P. Davies, of the Dragon, on the occasion of their diamond-wedding anniversary in March 1938. Three hunts, the Tanatside, the United and Mr. Hulton Harrop's met to honour the event. In the photograph, to the left of Alderman C.P. Davies are Mr. de Courcy Parry and Mr. Harry George and to the right of Mrs. Davies, Lord Powis, Captain Brierley and Mr. Jack Davies

known to have met in Montgomery. Traditionally the meet assembled outside the Dragon Hotel. C.P. Davies, who was the landlord between 1912 and 1941, was an enthusiastic life-long supporter:

> It is his boast that he has followed fox and stag, otter and hare for 60 years, under every master of hounds Montgomeryshire has had during that time.[1]

To celebrate the occasion of his Diamond Wedding anniversary there was a large and colourful gathering of the three hunts in front of the hotel.

Among other country pursuits, there was hare coursing at Lymore, and Mr. Buckley's Otter Hounds met near the Station 'weather and water permitting'. In 1869 the landlord of the Checkers Hotel, C. Davies, was breeding greyhounds. There are records of horse races being held on the Flôs lands in 1841 and on Lymore Meadow on Show Days. Prize fighting was one of the main attractions at the May Fair. Cockfighting was always extremely popular and much trouble was taken in breeding and preparing birds for battle, for a

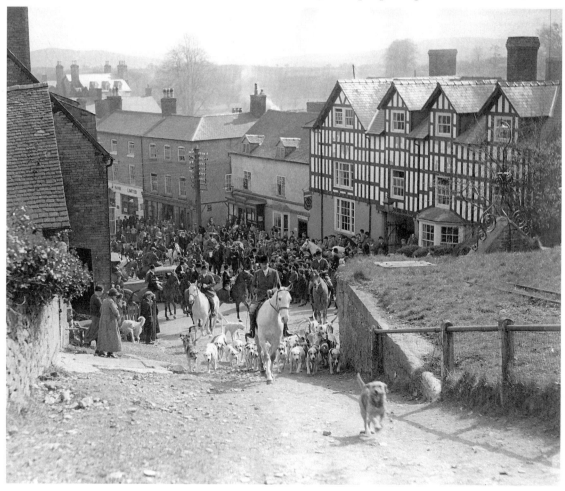

The hunts leaving the Dragon, March 1938

A foot pack, probably David Davies, who often met mid-week outside the Dragon Hotel with C.P. Davies in the centre, c.1910

considerable amount of money was won and lost in wagers on the outcome of the fights. An old cockpit lay behind the Lion Hotel at Caerhowel on the track leading down to the river Severn, and two further cockpits can be found on the way up to Town Hill. The first is a hundred yards up from the wicket gate opposite the Old Castle Farm and close by the town wall, and the other, once known as the Bowl, is hidden, up to the right of the track, through the trees.

Evidence of the variety of children's games played in Montgomery has been found both by gardeners and by archaeologists. Marbles, spinning tops, dice and perhaps most interesting of all, a Nine Men's Morris board[2] have all been dug up in cottage gardens throughout the town. Skipping, hoops and hopscotch were popular,

A Prize Fight in the early 1900s

143

Two of the Powell boys boxing in their back yard behind Chapel Place

and as the boys grew older they begged pigs' bladders from the butcher. Pigs used to be killed when they had reached a much heavier weight than is the case now, and the bladder, which was blown up using a straw, made a very tidy ball to kick about.

Of all the games played in Montgomery, it is likely that football has the longest history, but there is little documented information before the second half of

Crowds watching a cockfight in the Bowl above the track leading to Town Hill

An early cup winning Montgomery football team with Charlie Statham, centre back row and G. Maddox and Howard Withers to the captain's left and W. Tanner and B. Maddox to his right

the 1800s when the Football Association set out formal rules. For many centuries prior to this the game was played in towns and villages through the streets. It was a very rough and ready affair with opposing teams endeavouring to propel the ball from one point in the town to another. In some communities the Shrove Tuesday 'game' was tantamount to an affray, with many injuries and old scores being settled. Maybe because of its disreputable reputation,

An early photograph of Montgomery football team, c.1890

Middle photograph: In the 1908-9 season the Montgomery Town team were winners of the Montgomeryshire Challenge Cup. Photograph taken in the Town Hall

Bottom photograph:
There has been traditional rivalry between those living at the top of town and those living at the bottom of town, the dividing line being the Pound. The rival teams are seen in this photograph.
L to R back row: George Oliver, Matthew Helme (Headmaster), Reg Jones, J.E. Tomley, Maurice Jones.
3rd row: Buster Trow, Ivor Tanner, Douglas Turnbull, Jim Evans, Tommy Whittingham, T. Weaver, James Turnbull.
2nd row: David Griffiths, Billy Whittingham, Harry Williams, ? Hoddy, Glyn Tanner, Arthur Davies, Chesley Withers, Selwyn Bishop, Hugh Vaughan.
Front row: David Jones, Billy Williams, C. Bryan Williams, Gordon Evans, Tommy Davies

The Montgomery Football team which reached the final of the Montgomeryshire Challenge Cup in 1937. They lost 4-0 to Newtown

1959 Montgomery Town, once again Montgomeryshire Challenge Cup winners. Photographed in the Spar Garden, Broad Street.
L to R standing: Brinley Robinson (Manager), Brian Pugh, Bernard Tanner, John Thomas, Brian Bolderston, Tom Pugh, Geoff Windsor (Captain).
L to R sitting: John Griffiths, Gordon Evans, Emlyn Morgan, Rowland Andrew, John Jones

football was late in gaining sponsorship. By 1879 matches were being reported quite regularly in the local newspapers[3] and in 1899 Montgomery Town joined the Welshpool Junior League.[4] The first organised games took place in Lymore Meadow where the Show is now held and the pitch would have been marked out and goal posts erected on the day of the match. Changing rooms are quite a recent innovation, and until they were built players used the Checkers or the Institute after the game. The club has had two particularly successful seasons, fifty years apart. In the 1909 final of the Montgomeryshire Challenge Cup, when they were very much the underdogs, they

Members of the Bowling Club in the 1950s with a visiting team

beat Llanidloes 1 - 0, and in 1959, they beat Llanymynech 3 - 0 to bring home the cup for the second time. Ned Evans who lived in Chirbury Road played in the first game, and Gordon, one of his three sons, scored the first goal in the 1959 match. The football club has thrived and now has its own established ground with a pavilion and a small stand for spectators.

Both bowling and cricket were generally regarded as respectable sports and attracted the patronage of the gentry long before football. It has been claimed that the Bowling Club in Montgomery is the oldest in Wales. In the club's records, an account dated 1773 lists the expenses for the 'Repairing and Fitting up Montgomery Bowling Green by Order of the Countess of Powis'. Amongst other expenses for labour and materials are:

To Bowls which Mr. Probert paid for in London	£2.16.0
To for Carriage of the Bowls from London and Salop	£0. 1. 4

In the Lymore Estate schedule and map of 1785, the Bowling Green and House are listed as 'kept for the accommodation of the Gentlemen'. The plan shows the Green to be on exactly the same site as it is today.

A very ancient code of rules, handed down over the years, has survived amongst the club's records. This document, entitled Orders at Bowling,[5] is not dated, but the hand-writing and the paper suggest the existence of a 'club' in the seventeenth century. The Rules are remarkably similar, despite the passage of time, to those drawn up when Drake was playing his famous game on Plymouth Hoe in 1588:

RULES OF THE GAME

1 That every man, a bowler, shall at his leaving ye green pay ye bowle keeper sixpence.

2 If any one stand between block and bowle, or within three yards of ye block, being once fairly warned to ye contrary, shall pay ye greenkeeper for every offence sixpence.

3 Ye standing shall be made where ye block is taken up within three yards by ye then leader, unless he goe directly back, then at his own discretion soe, yet doe not overmarke ye adverse partie.

4 If a bowle runing be stopt by ye adverse partie, or better upon ye side, then ye bowle is to be layd at ye blockhead.

5 If any player or other by his descretion take up block or bowle, before he cast or casts shall be granted, he shall loose ye cast to ye adverse partie.

6 If he that is last at block lift it up or cauze it to be taken up before ye adverse partie hath thrown ye last bowle he and his side shall loose ye cast at mark.

7 If a bowle be caste in anothers turne ye same bowle may be stopt runing by ye not by ye side that hurld it.

8 It shall be lawful for such men only to shew ground as are either bowlers or bettors that very game.

9 If a runing bowle be stopt or fowled by his own partie then that bowle is to be taken away.

10 If anyone shall disturb his bowle not touching ye trigge by his foot on ye same it shall be lawfull for ye adverse partie to stop that bowle from runing and make him throw again but is unlawfull for ye side that hurled that bowle to stop it.

11 All bowlers, bettors and spectators are to keepe their standing while ye bowles are runing and not follow, neither shall he or they doe anything that is prejudishal or advantageous, with wind, hatt or foot or otherwise. He only that has thrown ye bowle may follow his bowle at a yard distance, but no nearer.

12 If it be a dead caste he that did fling ye last caste or his partie shall hand ye leading of ye block.

13 No caste is to be measured before ye bowles be all hurled, but by ye consent of both sides.

14 If any gamester shall cast his adversary's bowle it shall be lawfull for any of ye contrary partie to stopp ye said bowle from runing and cause him to throw his own bowle.

15 If any lying bowle be removed out of its place by any bettor or spectator the same shall be replaced by indifferent men where it first was and he that removed ye same shall forfeit to ye greenkeepere 2d.

15 If any shall fling stickes, strawes or other thing that may hinder ye runing of ye bowles they shall pay for every time so doeing to greenkeeper 2d.

16 If anyone shall wilfully stoppe a bowle runing he shall pay ye game and betts or if by chance he shall pay ye greenkeeper 12d.

17 Whether by lott or match the rubbers (which is not to be lesse than 6d rubbers) is to be held and played out. And in case it comes to be game and game each the third game is to decide ye rubbers for ye whoie. All bettors accepted in ye rubbers game to bowle their charge, whether they hold double single or at all.

Preserved with this document were fifteen pages torn from a manuscript book containing entries of the minutes of the club between 1778 and 1809. The first entry is headed 'Montgomery, 1st July 1778' and reads:

> We whose names are hereunto subscribed do voluntarily agree to become members of the Bowling Green Society in the Town and to subscribe five shillings each toward the support of the game.

The first name on the list is that of the Earl of Powis, who subscribed five guineas, followed by twenty-three names each of whom gave five shillings.

An entry on 7 May 1793 reads:

> We do further agree that every member of this society who does not dine at the opening and close of the Green shall pay half a crown into the hands of the steward for each default, otherwise be expelled. We do also agree that no child shall be permitted to come on the Green and that the steward take proper measures to prevent any person from hanging clothes on the Bowling Green hedge.

At an annual meeting of the subscribers to the Green held at the Dragon Inn on 8 June 1801, the following were noted as present: 'Mr. Tanner - in the chair, Rev. M.E. Lloyd, Mr. Thos. Jones Lymore, Mr. Edye, Mr. C.G. Humphreys, Mr. Davies of Brompton'. The substance of the following rules for the future management of the Green were then unanimously resolved upon:

1   The Green shall open on the 4th day of June in every year, upon which day the members shall dine together at the Dragon Inn - at 2 o'clock p.m. when the President shall report the state of the accounts and all other matters relating to the Green. Every member not attending this meeting shall forfeit 2s. 6d. to the fund.
2   At this meeting a President shall be elected for the current year and also a Steward who shall act under the control of the President and be allowed 1 guinea per annum for his trouble. It shall be the Steward's duty to keep the Green - summer house - bowls & fence in respectable order, and also to enter minutes, write and send cards of invitation, keep the keys & accounts and report the latter monthly to the President together with all trespasses and other infractions of the Rules of the Green.
3   Thursday in every week shall be considered a publick day - when the Steward shall open the gate at 4 o'clock p.m. - & have an active boy ready to attend the gentlemen who bowl.
4   No person shall be permitted to bowl unless introduced by a member.
5   Each member shall pay 2s. 6d. annually towards the expenses of the Green and shall be deemed to continue a member until he gives notice to the contrary.
6   The green shall close upon the Thursday after Michaelmas Day.

It was also unanimously resolved that 'Revd. M.E. Lloyd shd be President and John Poundley, Steward for the current year 1801', which offices they respectively accepted.

An early picture of tennis players on the bowling green

Sir Harmood-Banner presenting the Montgomery Tennis Club cups in the 1930s

The newly built tennis court at the Hollies above the Kerry Road

In May 1894 the Town Council approached Lord Powis' agent, Mr. W. Forrester-Addie, asking whether 'Lord Powis would allow the Town Council to become tenants of the Bowling Green for the benefit of the Town'. With a reply in the affirmative the council framed rules for the management and letting of the Green. The Bowling Club, as it is now, was founded.

The poor Green keeper must have had a hard time maintaining the Green in the early days as it was frequently used for dances and children's sports. In September 1894, during the Harvest Festival, there was dancing on the Green and the church provided teas. On Friday 4 September 1896 the first of the annual Montgomery Horticultural Shows was held there. In May of the following year, the Bowling Club made an application to the council to allow tennis as well as bowls to be played on the Green. This was granted and the Bowls and Tennis Club came into being. It was not, however, until 1950 that the members wrote to the council requesting a meeting with them to discuss the possibility of securing additional land for proper tennis courts. Up until then tennis had been played on the

Montgomery Cricket team and their visitors in the late 1800s. The two umpires and scorer together with a Jack Russell can be seen. (Many pictures of early Montgomery cricket teams seem to feature one of these small dogs)

Green and on private courts at Clawdd-y-dre, The Hollies, Tre Llydiart, Stalloe Farm and Caerhowel Hall. In 1955 the Town Council succeeded in purchasing the Green for the sum of £150 from Powis Estates, along with adjoining land to accommodate two tennis courts.

From the site overlying the old town wall and nestling beneath the church, a succession of bowls and tennis players would have had an unsurpassed view of Lymore Hall before it was demolished, with the cricket ground just beyond.

Montgomery Cricket Team with visitors, c.1910

In the early 1800s it was common practice for wealthy landowners to have their own private cricket ground close to their country house. They would raise teams from among their tenants, together with paid professionals, to play against other wealthy neighbours, often for high stakes. As the years went by, the team playing at Lymore came to represent the town and eventually the Montgomery Cricket Club became established. The *Shrewsbury Chronicle* reported a game between 'eleven gentlemen of Montgomery and eleven of Newtown' on 17 September 1847.

There is an early record of a fiercely competed match which took place at Lymore on Friday 25 July 1851 when, in a two innings contest against a Llanidloes eleven, Montgomery won by one run! The original score sheets for this game survive to this day.[6] The club became more formally established by 1869 with the Rev. M. Lloyd as President, and went on to become very successful.

A few years later, the enthusiastic and highly efficient John Thistle became secretary and was very assiduous in producing the fixture list and informing the local press about results and forthcoming games. At the 1879 Annual General Meeting at the Checkers, John Thistle made the following appeal:

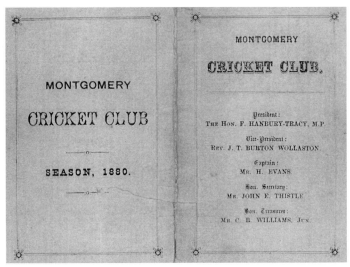

The club's fixture card 1880

Montgomery Cricket Club.

DATE.	CLUB.	GROUND.	MONTGOMERY		OPPONENTS.	
			1st Inns.	2nd Inns.	1st Inns.	2nd Inns.
Saturday, May 8th..	Married v. Single	Montgomery	*Single won by 8 wkts.*			
Friday, June 4th..	Oswestry	Oswestry	129	–	75	21 for 7 w.
Wednesday, June 16th..	Aston-on-Clun	Aston-on-Clun	66	–	16	31
Saturday, June 26th..	Welshpool	Welshpool	*opponents failed to keep appointment*			
Friday, July 9th..	Machynlleth	Machynlleth	67	–	15	11
Saturday, July 17th..	Aston-on-Clun	Montgomery	*opponents failed to keep appointment*			
Saturday, July 24th..	Towyn	Towyn	70	–	66	16 for 1 w.
Friday, 30 Wednesday	Montgomeryshire Good Templars (with Bailey).		111	–	31	
Aug. 11th.	Machynlleth	Montgomery	101	32 for 2 w.	55	–
Friday, Aug. 13th.	Llanidloes	Do.	91	7 for 1 w.	69	25
Saturday, Aug. 14th.	Welshpool	Do.	*opponents failed 8 ume*			
Tuesday, Aug. 24th.	Towyn	Do.	D.			
Saturday, Sept. 4th.	Oswestry	Do.	D.			
Friday, Sept. 17th.	Llanidloes	Llanidloes	33	14	167	–
Saturday, Sept. 25th.	Married v. Single	Montgomery	*Single won easily*			

The club's fixture card 1880

Parties wishing to become members or honorary members will greatly oblige by sending in their names to the secretary as early as possible. As a large proportion of the members of the club are working men we sincerely trust that the gentry round will kindly subscribe and place our national pastime within reach of all.[7]

One well-publicised match took place over three days between 16 and 18 June 1882 between a United All England Eleven and Twenty-Two of Montgomery.[8] Marquees and stands were erected and the Newtown Brass and Reed Band was in attendance. In perfect weather, large crowds came to watch the game. The All England team scored 76 and 97 in their two innings, but Montgomery won by 62 runs with scores of 120 and 115. Towards the end of the nineteenth century, detailed accounts of most of the local matches could be read in the local papers. Among reports of the danger of war in the Transvaal, the *Montgomery County Times* of 30 September 1899 gave the account of Montgomery Cricket Club's closing match and their annual supper at the Checkers. Whilst the members were enjoying a 'toothsome spread', the chairman, Arthur Vaughan, in his address, mentioned that Lord Powis had given the club free use of the ground.

However, all did not go smoothly. In the late 1920s a serious disagreement broke out among members and as a result, cricket was not played at Lymore for several years. The team moved, taking their pavilion with them, to play on the pitch at Caerhowel Hall. By 1934 things had calmed down and the club returned to its old home. Lord Powis kindly gave permission for the old wooden pavilion to be positioned, on its return, near the old gardens of the Hall, but only on condition that it was painted dark green rather than black and white. The old pavilion remained in use until the 1970s when the present brick-built structure replaced it on the present site. Quite recently the ground was described as 'one of the prettiest I've visited anywhere in the world' by a former Test and county player who held the post of Director of Cricket Development in Wales; it certainly has a fine setting in

MONTGOMERY.

GRAND CRICKET MATCH (15TH, 16TH, AND 17TH).—"THE UNITED-ALL-ENGLAND ELEVEN" *v.* TWENTY-TWO OF THE MONTGOMERY CRICKET CLUB.—We have the pleasure of informing our readers that the eleven will be selected from the following well known players, viz.:—Messrs. W. R. Gilbert, L. M. Day, W. K. Pullin, C. M. Kennedy, S. H. Evershed, with Woof, Jupp, Humphrey, Pooley Platts, Foster, Shaw, Shrewsbury, and Pamham. As such a strong team is to appear, the twenty-two will have to be very good to make anything like a fight of it. We trust that the energetic committee of the Montgomery Cricket Club, will be rewarded for their enterprise by securing a success, and that there will be a large attendance to witness the match.

Announcement in the Montgomeryshire Express, *23 May 1882, of the important forthcoming match between Twenty-Two of the Montgomery Cricket Club and the United-All-England Eleven in June, the paper giving a full match report on 20 June*

1882 photograph showing the Montgomery team fielding against the All-England Eleven at Lymore. The band can be seen playing in the shade of the trees between the two marquees

Cricketers and their supporters outside the pavilion during the temporary move to Caerhowel,
c.1930

Lymore Park with its ancient oaks and distant view of the old county town of Montgomery with its church and castle.

Mixed hockey was being played in Montgomeryshire as far back as the 1870s. Before the turn of the century women in many towns and villages throughout the county were forming their own hockey teams and around this time Montgomery Ladies Hockey Club became established. Sadly, the early matches were not reported in the local papers but detailed accounts do survive in exercise books of spirited matches against neighbouring clubs. Local teams they played against included Newtown, Berriew, Forden, Chirbury and Churchstoke, and they also travelled as far as Llanfyllin, Machynlleth and UCW Aberystwyth. There are some splendid photographs of the early teams showing the extraordinary dress worn by the players. It is difficult to imagine how the ladies managed even to run, never mind play hockey, wearing a long skirt containing several yards of flannel worn over a full petticoat. The pictures show the elaborate hairstyles and narrow waists, as small as sixteen inches in circumference, and requiring stays. As the game progressed on the muddy pitches the skirts became increasingly heavy as they dragged in the dirt. Despite these handicaps the games were all very keenly contested. The women have

Montgomery Cricket Team, c.1925
L to R back row: Gethin, Harold Turnbull, Fred Caine, Bert
Howard, Malcolm Kinsey, Ernie Weaver, Bert Davies.
Front row: Maitland Taylor, J.E. Tomley, Rev. W.E. Jones,
W.W. Vaughan, Silas Hamer, Reg Jones, John Roberts

Montgomery Cricket Team in the middle 1930s
L to R standing: Ernie Weaver, Walter Wood, Arthur
Cobbold, ? , Jack Davies (Well House), Harry Edwards,
Arthur Withers.
Seated: Reg Jones, Edwin Jones (Rev.), Tom Kilvert,
Fred Weaver.
In front: Ron Perry and Allan Bunner

never had a permanent pitch for their games, sometimes playing on the same fields used for football, sometimes on the field at the corner of Pool Road and New Road, and occasionally on the cricket pitch. This has not deterred them and Montgomery continues to have an enthusiastic and active ladies team.

Lymore Park was the setting for at least two other sporting activities. A nine-hole golf course was briefly in existence in the early 1900s behind the Hall on the 'Windy Oaks' fields.

In severe winters, when the lower pool at Lymore freezes over, the town is provided with a wonderful skating rink. Basil Phillips, the bachelor son of a vicar of Kerry, who lodged in Kerry Street, was always relied

Montgomery Ladies Hockey Team, c.1909. Rose Williams, the captain,
stands at the back on the right

155

*Montgomery Ladies Hockey team, 1933
L to R standing: Edna Holloway, Phyllis Davies, May
Holloway, Joan Statham, Patsy Davies, Marjory Jones.
Sitting: Doris Berwick, Mary Williams, Cissy Tanner,
Margaret Gornall, Clara James*

upon to decide if and when it was safe to venture on
to the ice. In a time when everyone wore lace up
boots it was not difficult to screw or strap simple iron
skates to the thick leather soles. From the pictures
taken by David Proctor, it would appear that a high
proportion of the population of the town enjoyed
skating and playing hockey on the frozen pool in the
days when every winter seemed to be long and hard.

*Lymore Pool was frequently frozen
hard in the winter months providing
free fun for the townsfolk of
Montgomery. David Proctor's picture
shows many out skating and playing
hockey, c.1910*

*The opening of the golf course on the Windy Oaks field at Lymore by Mrs. Price-Davies of
Marrington. The stout gentleman on the left, wearing a hat is Dr. Kirk, c.1905*

15 Celebrations and Events

Communities have always gathered together at certain times in the year to celebrate specific occasions. In pagan times, the midsummer solstice was observed with highly complex rituals and with the spread of Christianity, Easter and Christmas became important dates in the calendar. The changing seasons, particularly in rural areas, brought about annual events such as the Hiring Fairs in the spring and Harvest Festivals in the autumn. Every town and village would look forward to its own particular annual round of events. In Montgomery the pattern of many of these has survived down the years to the present day.

The first Thursday in May is the date in Montgomery's calendar that has always been eagerly anticipated by most people, although some viewed the day with apprehension. Originally known as the Hiring and Pleasure Fair, it was the day when 'hands' were hired by farmers. As the years went by, it became simply a pleasure fair,

The harvesters joined by members of the Proctor and Lucas families enjoying a well earned picnic, c.1910

Montgomery ladies taking afternoon tea in the garden, c.1910

known as the May Fair and is described in more detail on pp.81-85. In June and July both children and adults enjoyed the trips organised by the chapels, the church and the National School, usually to the seaside. The favourite destination was Aberystwyth and special trains for the parties were booked from Montgomery station. Picnics and tea parties with sports were arranged as treats for the children by a variety of benevolent organisations and generous individuals.

Show Day is another event in which the whole town takes part with great enthusiasm. Following a very successful Flower Show on the Bowling Green on Friday 6 September 1895, the Montgomery & District Horticultural Society was founded and a year later staged their first show, again using the Bowling Green. Later, and until the late 1930s, it was held on a Thursday in August on Lymore Meadow and was a very grand affair. There were as many as three marquees, along with livestock displays, military bands, professional entertainers and horse racing in adjacent fields. After the war the show was held on Clos Tanymur, then for several years in the Town Hall and more recently has moved back to Lymore Meadow. These days it takes place on the third Saturday in August and continues to be a highly popular occasion when families and past Montgomery residents often return to visit old friends and relatives. Traditionally, the evening of 'Show Day' ended with a frantic confetti battle in Broad Street, in which everyone took part. To the disappointment of many, the local council decided to ban the 'battle' after the 1965 Show following complaints from the street cleaners about the extra work involved in clearing up the resulting litter.

In autumn, after the harvest has been gathered in,

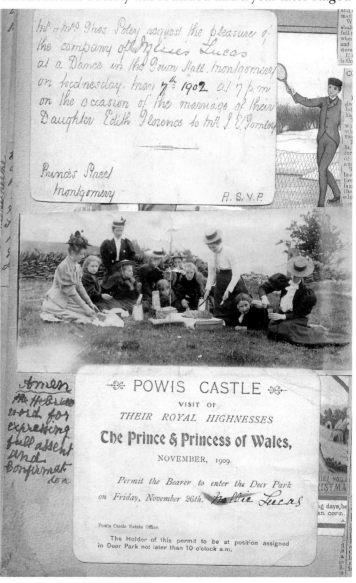

A page from a Lucas family scrapbook. Family picnics have always been popular

The Corndon Magazine (Church Monthly) for 1895 reported:

Arrangements are being made to hold a small Show on the Bowling Green, on Friday September 6th to encourage gardening amongst the Cottagers and others. Money prizes will be given for Flowers, Fruit and Vegetables grown and exhibited by Cottagers living in Montgomery and adjoining parishes whose rental does not exceed £8 per annum. Cards of Merit will also be awarded for the best exhibits shown by Farmers, Tradesmen and others. Full particulars will be found in the Schedules, which may be obtained from Mr. John Davies, Church Bank. Tea and refreshments will be provided on the ground, and a Band will play for Dancing. We hope that the parishioners and others will help this venture by exhibiting and patronising the Show.

Later the same year: Thanks to the energy of the promoters, the keenness of the exhibitors, the interest of the parishioners in the district, and especially to the kindness of the ladies and gentlemen who sent beautiful exhibits to embellish the tent, the Flower Show held on the bowling Green in Montgomery, on Friday, September 6th, was in every way a successful one ... We hope that we shall have another Flower Show next year, that it will be on the same ground, and at the same time, and that we shall have a fine day, and that it will be in every way as great a success as the first venture.

services of Thanksgiving are still held in the church and chapels, which are ornately bedecked with evergreens, flowers, sheaves of corn, fruit and vegetables. At first the produce was subsequently distributed to the 'deserving' poor, now, with less stigma, it is passed on to elderly parishioners. These services have always attracted some of the largest congregations of the year, and in the past were often followed by tea and sometimes by dancing on the 'Green'. In early winter, fund raising sales-of-work and fêtes took place, some lasting for two days.

The annual dinners for the various sporting clubs and other organisations usually took place in the winter months. After the meal and the speeches, dancing could go on well into the early hours of the morning, sometimes starting at the Bowling Green and then moving to the Town Hall. The Annual Church Christmas party held in the National Schoolroom on 26 December 1895 was:

Montgomery Show tent shortly after judging the horticultural exhibits, c.1910

The carnival floats in Broad Street on Show Day, c.1910.
The photograph was taken prior to the conversion of Pen-y-grisiau into a shop

The Young Farmers float at Montgomery Show with in the late 1940s. Amongst those present can be
seen Meurick Jones and two of his children, Court Calmore, Reg Jones, The Brades, Philip and
Clara Davies and their daughters, Philippa and Sheila, Stalloe, Clara's two sisters Ann and Mary
and Arthur Roberts, the Midland Bank

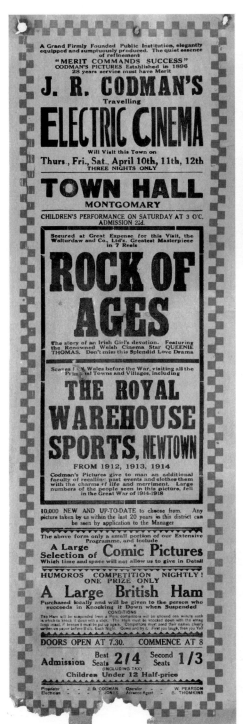

The Darby and Joan float at Montgomery Show in the early 1960s. Amongst those present can be seen Mr. and Mrs. Ned Evans, Plas Offa Cottages, Mrs. Jessie Sleigh, Rock House and Mrs. Tom Weaver

a great success. Excellent arrangements were made by the energetic committee of ladies ... dancing was kept up with great spirit to excellent music supplied by Mr. J.S. Keedwell until 4.00 am

After the Christmas festivities were over, the cold and dank winter months were enlivened by entertainment in the Town Hall, Chapel Schoolroom and School. There were concerts with piano and violin solos and duets, operatic arias, glee songs, patriotic songs and other such entertainment all performed by the local residents. Live entertainment has and always will be enjoyed, and undoubtedly the most enduring and well-known feature of the Montgomery music scene over the past sixty or so years has been Ivor Tanner's band. The group came into being during the last war with Ivor playing lead trumpet and drums, Doris Parry the piano, Gordon Evans accordion and many more talented musicians on a variety of other instruments over the years. They became very well known and performed at many dances, weddings and other functions as far away as Leominster, Aberystwyth and Shrewsbury and are still to be heard in their regular sessions in the Dragon Hotel.

1924 poster for J.R. Codman's travelling Electric Cinema and other entertainments in the Town Hall

*Poster for the Odd Fellows Concert in
the Town Hall in 1842*

*Ivor Tanner's Band playing at Powis Castle in 1978 on
the occasion of the Knights of St. John Ball.
Playing are L to R: Paddy Clarke and Christopher Pryce -
lead and rhythm guitars, Ivor Tanner - trumpet,
Arnold Horton - saxophone, Cadfan Evans - drums,
Doris Parry- keyboard, Stuart Tanner - bass guitar*

Magic lantern slide shows were very popular in Victorian times and were replaced by silent movies and eventually a regular weekly film show in the Town Hall. The Penny Readings also held in the Town Hall every fortnight were very well attended in the winter evenings. In 1894, one elderly resident claimed that she could remember, some thirty years before, counting 618 people, young and old, present in one crowded house. Surely an exaggeration but they did survive for many years, a measure of their popularity.

Montgomery has always relished the excuse for a stylish celebration, but undoubtedly, the rejoicing in honour of the coming-of-age of the Viscount Clive in November 1839 must have been the longest and most extravagant on record:

Right: Town Hall Entertainment Programme 1919

North Wales Heroes' Memorial
Entertainment

Town Hall. Montgomery,
JANUARY 15th and 16th, 1919.

Programme.

Having amply supplied the wants of the youngsters, and provided also for their evening's amusement with innocent diversions, the Committee, and a numerous party of friends repaired to the Dragon Inn, where "mine host," Mr. Read, had provided an excellent dinner. The chair was taken by Sir C. T. Jones. Due honor was done to the numerous toasts proposed, more especially the toast of the day, which was most vehemently responded to.

In the course of the evening the poor women of the parish (upwards of 150) were regaled with tea, qualified with French and Jamaica cream. At night a flight of sky-rockets was discharged from Broad Street, and another from the Town Hill as a prelude to a splendid display of fire-works. Two immense bon-fires also sent forth their cheering rays from the top of the Town Hill, and continued blazing throughout the night. A dance at the Chequers concluded the festivities of Tuesday.

On Wednesday the festivities were renewed. Early in the morning crowds were seen wending their merry way towards Broad Street, where a procession was forming, to parade two magnificent beeves and several fine fat sheep, on waggon platforms, through the town and its suburban districts. The procession (enlivened by numerous banners, flags, &c., bearing appropriate mottoes) was accompanied by the Montgomery band, playing appropriate airs in good style. Having gratified the residents in the various streets with a sight of the cavalcade, the party returned to the Town Hall, where

the beeves and sheep were cut up, and distributed in liberal portions, with a suitable quantity of bread, to all the resident poor. Nor was "*Old Tempest*" forgotten; for the Earl of Powis kindly sent a barrel to the Committee to be given away upon the occasion. Immediately after the distribution of meat, every one of the numerous assemblage took "*a right gude willy whack*" of this celebrated old stingo towards the health of the heir to the Powis estates.

The Committee had other claims upon their attention. It formed part of the arrangement at Montgomery, and a very laudable one too, that the soldiers stationed in the town (a detachment of the gallant 12th, under the command of Captain Reid,) as also the prisoners in the County Gaol should not, upon this festive occasion, be forgotten. In accordance, therefore, with this praiseworthy resolution, a fine fat sheep, together with bread, *Old Tempest*, &c., in most bountiful proportions, were sent to the barracks for the soldiery; and another, with suitable accompaniments, to the county prison for the inmates there.

Parts of two pages from An Account of Rejoicings in the Counties of Montgomery, Salop etc. in honor of the Coming-of-age of The Viscount Clive, November 5th 1839

The good people of Montgomery were eagerly anxious for the arrival of the long looked for 5th of November, as affording them an opportunity of pouring out their grateful feelings, their warmest congratulations to the earl and Countess of Powis, and the Viscount Clive, at so momentous, so auspicious period, as that in which the youthful heir to such vast possessions merged into manhood.[1]

On the day, a Tuesday, the people of Montgomery were

aroused from their slumbers by the firing of cannon, and a merry peal from the beautiful church tower ... at seven o'clock, a numerous procession, headed by a band in an open carriage, with flags and banners bearing mottoes, formed opposite the Guildhall, and proceeded from thence to Powis Castle, with addresses of congratulation to the Earl and Countess of Powis and the Viscount Clive.

The procession then returned to Montgomery 'to superintend the festivities of the day'. In fact the merry making was to last for the rest of the week.

Street parties and bonfires have been a feature of every Coronation and Jubilee over the last century and probably well before. The first to be recorded photographically was Queen Victoria's Golden Jubilee in June 1887 when it was celebrated with a procession and a special service in the church, followed by dinner for more than 800 adults in Broad Street and tea for the children

Street Party to celebrate the Queen Victoria's Golden Jubilee in 1887.
The photograph was taken by J. Owen of Newtown

A bonfire, at this stage, five men high, being built on Town Hill to celebrate the Coronation of George V on 23 June 1911—as discovered when the poster to the right of the men on the ladder was sufficiently enlarged!

in the National Schoolroom. Sports and dancing took place in Lymore Park and dancing was later continued in the Town Hall with fireworks to follow. Apparently the only drawback to the day was the intolerable heat. It was not surprising that this was commented on, for the photograph above taken by Mr. John Owen of Newtown shows the heavy, formal clothing then *de rigeur* for such events. Festivities had started the previous evening with the lighting of a monstrous beacon on Town Hill at 10 o'clock with the signal of a rocket from Corndon. With cheers, Her Majesty's health was toasted with the liberal supply of ale for the 1,000 people on the hill. The National Anthem was sung and then followed more fireworks and 'cannon' fire.

Crowds in Broad Street celebrating the Coronation of George V, 23 June 1911.
Most of the children can be seen to be wearing their coronation medals

Street party held to celebrate the end of the First World War, 1919

'Cannon' fire was not only reserved for 'state' occasions. When the then Town Clerk, Charles Sidney Pryce, and his bride returned from their honeymoon in 1892 and passed under the decorated arches and Chinese lanterns, 'they were greeted with cheering and cannon fire by the large and effusive crowd'. Celebrations for the wedding continued over the next day with sports in Broad Street and dancing till the early hours. Schoolchildren were given a day's holiday to allow them to join in. Another notable wedding was that of Betty Harmood-Banner, the daughter of Sir Harmood Harmood-Banner, on Tuesday 18 August 1931. Sir Harmood, who lived at Caerhowel Hall in the parish, was Mayor from 1928 to 1931 and a keen supporter of the cricket and tennis clubs. The large attendance at the ceremony can be judged by the number of expensive chauffeur driven cars filling Broad Street. The *County Times* reported:

The George V Jubilee celebrations in Broad Street, 6 May 1935. Amongst those to be seen in the photograph are the Mayor, Dr. J.D.K. Lloyd, his brother Dr. Wyndham Lloyd, Dr. S.J. Stewart and Betty and Rachel, the Grosvenor-Launder twins

Prince Charles visiting Montgomery Castle on the morning of Friday 3 June 1977 accompanied by Dr. J.D.K. Lloyd, Ivor Tanner and the Mayor, Tecwyn Davies. He was then granted the Freedom of the Borough and opened an exhibition in the school recording Montgomery's long history. There followed a week of celebrations to commemorate the 750th anniversary of the granting of the first charter to Montgomery in 1223

Broad Street lined with chauffeur driven cars on the occasion of the marriage of Betty Harmood-Banner of Caerhowel Hall, 18 August 1931

The school log book entry showing the excitement at the Fall of Pretoria in 1900. In those days most newsworthy information was announced outside the Town Hall to the gathering crowds

Not for many years has a public event so stirred the ancient county town. For some time before the wedding the townspeople were busy making elaborate preparations, and on the day of the happy event the town was quite *en fête* to do honour to its civic chief and his winsome daughter who has been a popular figure in local society.

After the service the choirboys were each presented with a pound—more money than any of them had ever possessed at any one time!

Schoolchildren gathered outside the Town Hall to hear the proclamation of George V in 1910. The school log book records:- 'May 9 1910 The children assembled, and the Registers were marked as usual, but before the closing of the Registers a message was received from the Mayor [N.W. Fairles Humphreys] asking that the children should be marched into Broad St. to hear read the proclamation of the New King, George V. The attendance marks were cancelled, as a half-holiday was given in commemoration of the event'

Starting on Sunday 31 July 1927 the town celebrated the 700th anniversary of the granting of the royal charter (this page and opposite)

Lord Clive, the Mayor, C.S. Pryce and the Earl of Powis leaving the Town Hall by the back entrance. This was the main entrance in those days

The Earl of Powis and Lord Clive in the procession along Broad Street

Beginning of the march from the Town Hall to Lymore Park

The pageant depicting the four gates and the seasons with the Montgomery banner in the centre

The town celebrating the 700th anniversary of the granting of the royal charter

Procession led by the Borough Band advancing up Pool Road

Members of the cricket club dressed in costume outside the Checkers

Montgomery town stocks with two local ruffians imprisoned, for fun. (Allan Bunner and Fred Pryce)

Town Hill with the newly erected Montgomeryshire County War Memorial in 1923

One particularly memorable occasion took place only twenty-six years ago and is still fresh in the minds of many Montgomery folk. For a week in June 1977, which coincided with the Queen's Silver Jubilee, the whole town indulged itself in commemorating the 750th Anniversary of the granting of the royal charter by Henry III in 1227. On the Friday prior to the week, the Prince of Wales spent most of the day in the town after being presented with the Honorary Freedom of the Borough. During Charter Week, as it came to be called, there were pageants, street parties, concerts, balls and hog roasts. Many citizens were dressed in medieval costume for the whole week. The exhibition in the school, displaying the

23 April 1923 saw all who could get there, by whatever means, joining in a service of dedication of the County War Memorial

long history of Montgomery, attracted over 2,000 visitors and laid the foundations for the development of the Old Bell Museum several years later. Still in the memory of some of the older members of the community are the 700th Charter celebrations of 1927, which, as the pictures show, were just as elaborate and equally enjoyed.

The Town Hall was the place in the town where citizens gathered to learn the important national news of the day. Deaths and accessions of monarchs, famous military victories such as the news of the Relief of Mafeking, announcements signalling the ending of the two World Wars and results of elections were all announced to large crowds. These frequently included all the school-children who were marched down to Broad Street for these special occasions.

To commemorate the men from Montgomeryshire who lost their lives in the Great War the Town Hill, with its wide views of Mid Wales, was chosen as the site for the County War Memorial. A service of dedication was held there on 23 April 1923. The monument, of Portland stone, a landmark for miles around, suffered serious structural damage from an earthquake in 1990 and has recently has been

A service of re-dedication of the County War Memorial was held on a windy October day in 2002. Standing in front of the monument is Terry Boundy who was largely instrumental in raising funds for its restoration, and to his right are Arthur Baldwin, Arthur Tanner and Verdun Gornall

Queen Elizabeth II being welcomed to Montgomery by the Mayor, Councillor Madge Richards on Friday 11 July 1986 during her tour of Powys

restored. A very moving and well-attended rededication service took place on Saturday 5 October 2002 when the work had been completed. A new tablet was unveiled which reads:

THIS MEMORIAL COMMEMORATES
ALL THOSE PEOPLE FROM THE
COUNTY OF MONTGOMERYSHIRE
WHO GAVE THEIR LIVES IN ALL WARS

There is no record of a reigning monarch visiting Montgomery since Henry III in the thirteenth century until Queen Elizabeth II came on Friday 11 July 1986 during a visit to Powys.

Broad Street has been the scene of numerous celebrations. Of recent times it has become the tradition, on New Year's Eve, just before midnight, that nearly the whole population, together with visiting friends and relatives, pour into the street from every doorway, link arms to form a huge circle and sing 'Auld Lang Syne'.

16 Photographers

In a time when digital photography is rapidly becoming popular, films in sealed cassettes can be developed and printed in less than an hour and some cameras are totally disposable, it is easy to forget the difficulties facing the early photographers. Their cameras were bulky and heavy, invariably requiring a tripod. The glass plates were delicate and difficult to store—one quarter plate taking up more space that a modern digital flash card containing hundreds of images. The processing of plates, using chemicals as toxic as potassium cyanide, was complicated, messy and dangerous. Despite the problems, however, many of the photographs taken can stand comparison with those of today.

Only brief mention has been made to the photographers, both professional and amateur, whose pictures have been used to illustrate this book. David Proctor lived next to the Town Hall in Arthur Street where he ran a general store. He was an extremely able photographer whose collection of glass plates has provided the town with a priceless archive. Several hundred of these were rescued from the attic when the building changed hands in the 1970s. He took numerous photographs of his family and the town, many of which were made into postcards. On the opposite side of Arthur Street, the solicitor J.E. Tomley dabbled quite seriously in photography producing some fine results. A large number of his glass plates are still in existence. His partner C.S. Pryce was another skilled amateur photographer, many of whose plates sadly were destroyed by vandals whilst in store in Welshpool in the early 1970s, some however have survived. The other important collection of pictures came from the Powell family who lived at the bottom of Arthur Street. It has not been possible to identify which member actually took the photographs most of which are of family and friends. Although the majority of the illustrations come from the above sources, a significant number have come from personal collections when the actual photographer is not known.

In the early days of photography, long exposures were the rule, requiring the subject to remain very still while the picture was being taken. This often resulted in very stiff, formal and somewhat daunting looking portraits. All the above photographers seem to have been quite adventurous and have taken many informal, unposed pictures. Some of these and others that have not fitted comfortably into the chapters are of such interest and quality that to omit them would be regrettable. The following collection of pictures from many different sources all display the skill and imagination of the photographers and allow the observer to look back to a time now long forgotten.

J.E. Tomley, the photographer in action

This picture, dated July 1893 on the back, was taken by an unknown itinerant photographer who had set up his American Studio in front of Rock house behind the Town Hall. He has recorded the flooding resulting from a severe cloudburst that has nearly washed the road away

The glass plate from which this photograph is taken was among a collection from J.E. Tomley's solicitors' office in Arthur Street. The make of the elegant car standing in front of the Gaol gateway has been identified as a Jackson made in 1912-13, in Notting Hill Gate, London. It may well have been the means of transport of either Dr. Reynolds or Dr. Robertson who practised from the Gaol

C.S. Pryce, another solicitor, took many photographs and was also a keen fisherman. Here he is after a good day with three fine trout. He has helpfully noted down their weight and date of capture: 3^1/$_4$lbs, 4th April 1904

David Proctor provided many of the pictures in this book; he was, perhaps, the only person in Montgomery who can be regarded as a professional photographer. The detail in this photograph of him as a young man, standing by the seat in the castle grounds, extensively carved with initials, is impressive

Florrie and Hilda, David Proctor's two pretty daughters posing for their Dad

Mr. & Mrs. David Proctor,
Florence and Hilda

Hilda and Florrie and their mother, Mrs. Proctor,
with two friends and motorbike in the yard
behind their house in Arthur Street

David Proctor took many
photographs outside, and
was not afraid of experi-
menting with different
conditions. This is a
winter view of the new
path to the castle

The motorcar has always attracted the attention of photographers. The 9HP Darracq with a tonneau cover, was painted dull grey with red wheels when first registered under the Motor Car Act 1903 on 13 June 1904. The first owner was a Mr. J.S. Brown of Swansea. It is parked in Chirbury Road outside Alexandria Terrace, which was built by Mr. William Brown who sold his ironmonger's business to R.H. Bunner

This photographic plate was found among David Proctor's collection. The date is uncertain and the identities of the two ladies perched on the railings fishing is unknown, but the scene is not unfamiliar. The car in the far distance is contemplating whether or not to attempt to cross the floods on the flat lands near the Kilkewydd Bridge on the road from Montgomery to Welshpool

This snapshot was taken on a glass plate (unfortunately cracked) of a fight near the Pound, from the attic window of the tailor's workshop at Chapel Place by a member of the Powell family

This photograph from Les Evans' family was somewhat puzzling. Some of the people could be identified but where and what was going on was unclear. In the centre holding a pick is Ned Evans and behind him, sitting, is his wife Louie with son Les and other children. Others in the picture are Jack Blower, Howard Withers and Frank Whittingham. The photograph below gave us the answer

A collection of glass plates from Tomley's offices contained two pictures that matched the previous snapshot. The skyline behind the excavations, showing the Callow and Corndon, identified the site as that of the town reservoir, which was built in 1937

*These three pictures show detail from the photographs of the markets in Montgomery around 1905.
They are unusual in that they are completely unposed*

*An early snapshot in Arthur Street, with David Proctor standing in the doorway
of his brother Dick's shop*

Postscript: a sylvan scene

References

Chapter 1 Introduction
1. *Archaeologia Cambrensis* XCVII, pp.1-57
2. *Hen Domen, Montgomery. Vol., I,* Philip Barker and Robert Higham, The Royal Archaeological Institute, 1982; *Hen Domen, Montgomery, A Final Report,* Philip Barker and Robert Higham, The Royal Archaeological Institute, University of Exeter Press, 2000
3. *Bloody Montgomery 1223-1295,* Paul M. Remfry, 1998
4. *Travels through England of Dr. Richard Pococke, successively Bishop of Meath and of Ossory, during 1750, 1751 and later years,* ed, James Joel Cartwright, Camden Society Publications, Vol II new series No 44, 1889
5. *A Tour in Wales, Vol. II,* Pennant, Printed by Henry Hughes, London, 1781
6. *The Complete English Traveller or a New Survey and description of England and Wales,* Nathaniel Spencer Esq. London, J.Cooke, 1771
7. *A short account of a journey into Wales,* Lord George Lyttleton in two letters written to Mr. Bower, undated Annual Register Vol XVII, 1774, NLW
8. *The Torrington Diaries containing the tours through England and Wales of the Hon. John Byng between the years 1781 and 1794, Vol I, Tour to North Wales,* John Byng
9. Letters Written during a Tour Through North Wales in 1798, Rev. J. Evans, NLW

Chapter 2 Town and Castle
1. *Archaeologia Cambrensis* CXLI, pp.97-180
2. *Montgomeryshire Collections* 59, pp.140-144
3. *Archaeologia Cambrensis* CXVII, pp.127-156
4. *Montgomeryshire Collections* 8, pp.313-334
5. *Montgomeryshire Express and Radnor Times,* 26 February 1924
6. *Montgomeryshire Collections* 66, pp.113-115
7. *North Wales Delineated from Two Excursions through all the interesting parts of that highly beautiful and romantic country, and intended as a guide to future tourists,* Rev. W. Bingley London, 2nd Ed. Longmans 1814 (tour of 1798)

Chapter 3 Church and Chapel
1. *Montgomeryshire Collections* 67, pp.7-44
2. *Montgomeryshire Collections* 56, pp.21-41
3. Letters, notebooks and correspondence belonging to the James and Davies family, late of Plas Offa, Montgomery
4. *Ibid.*
4. 'Borderland Methodism' in *The Methodist Recorder,* 30 Dec 1909

Chapter 4 Civic Life
1. *Montgomeryshire Collections* 36, pp.53-78
2. *Ibid.*
3. *Ibid.*
4. *Pridden's Topographical Collections, Monmouthshire and Wales*, by Rev. John Pridden, 1784
5. *Montgomeryshire Collections* 46, pp.22-25
6. *Montgomeryshire Express and Radnor Times* together with supplements, December 1892

Chapter 5 Lymore Hall
1. *Herbert Correspondence*, ed. W.J. Smith, Board of Celtic Studies, University of Wales, History & Law Series XXI, University of Wales Press, 1963
2. PRO, sc6 1206/3; early ref Lymore Park Leymore 1364/5 R A H
3. *Herbert Correspondence, op.cit.*
4. *Ibid.*
5. *The Official Progress of the Duke of Beaufort through Wales in 1684*, Thomas Dineley, N LW
6. Survey and Valuation of Lands belonging to the Earl of Powis in the Counties of Montgomery and Salop (1785), Powis Castle Estate Office
7. *Montgomeryshire Collections* 18, pp.155-168
8. *Pilgrimages to Old Homes mostly on the Welsh Border*, Fletcher Moss, 1903, pp.247-255
9. *The Last of Lymore*, Mary Newell Owen, supplement to *Montgomeryshire Express and Radnor Times*, Tuesday 29 October 1929
10. *Montgomeryshire Collections* 18, pp.155-168
11. *Montgomeryshire Collections* 45, p.101-3, and 47, p.4
12. *Montgomeryshire Collections* 42, pp.1-10

Chapter 6 Schools
1. Montgomeryshire Collections 30, pp.291-300
2. *Education in a Welsh rural County 1870-1973*, J.A. Davies, University of Wales Press, 1973
3. Reports of the Commissioners of Enquiry into the State of Education in Wales, Part III, London, HMSO 1847
4. Montgomery School Log Books 1865 onwards

Chapter 7 Markets and Fairs
1. *Montgomeryshire Collections* 21, pp.1-34
2. *Montgomeryshire Collections* 65, pp.13-17
3. *Ibid.*
4. Tape Talks to the Blind, Old Bell Museum Archives
5. *Ibid.*
6. *Corndon Magazine*, Church Monthly, 1893
7. Tape Talks, *op.cit*

Chapter 8 Trades and Professions
1. Other Directories examined are *Pigot & Co.'s North Wales* 1844, *Slater's North Wales* 1868, *Worrall's* 1874, *Sutton's* 1889-90 and *Slater's North & Mid Wales* 1895.
2. *Oswestry Bye-gones*, 1885 p.309 (Montgomery Gaol File, 8 April 1650)
3. *A Montgomery Notebook*, Dr. J.D.K. Lloyd, 1971, p.47
4. Tape Talks for the Blind, The Old Bell Museum
5. Personal correspondence

Chapter 10 The Tanyard
1. *Montgomeryshire Collections* 49, pp.244-5
2. *A Montgomery Note-Book*, J.D.K. Lloyd, 1971, pp.25-7

Chapter 11 Clock and Watchmakers
1. *Clock and Watchmakers in Wales*, Iorwerth C. Peate, The National Museum of Wales, 1945

Chapter 12 The Gaol
1. *Chronicle of the Princes*, 1115
2. *Montgomeryshire Collections* 59, pp.140-144
3. 'That Ancient Servant of the Lord, Richard Davies', the Quaker from Welshpool, ?1666
4. *Fragmenta Antiquitatis or Ancient Tenures of Land and Jocular Customs of Some Manors*, Thomas Blount of the Inner-temple
5. Survey of Gaol, 26 Mar 1774, Powys Archives
6. John Howard, *The State of the Prisons Vol. 1*, p. 452 (4th Edition, 1792), NLW
7. Nield's Report, *Bye-gones*, 1878-1879, p.81 & p.92
8. Returns from John Davies Gaoler, Powys Archives
9. Thos. Edye, *Bye-gones*, 1878-1879, p.97
10. County Gaol Order Book 1804 -1837, Powys Archives
11. John Howard, *op.cit.*
12. *Salopian Journal*, 18 and 25 August 1830, Shrewsbury Local Studies Library
13. *Topographical Directory of Wales*, 4th Ed., Samuel Lewis, London, 1849
14. County Gaol Order Book, *op.cit.*

Chapter 13 Fire Service
1. From Mrs. G.M. Davies' childhood memories of Montgomery, Old Bell Museum Archives
2. This information comes from the first minute book of the newly formed fire brigade, Old Bell Museum Archives
3. *From Horses to Helicopters. Some notes on fire service history, with particular reference to the fire stations in the counties of Denbigh and Monmouthshire* by D. Wheway Davies, pp.112-114

Chapter 14 Sports and Pastimes
1. *The Montgomery County Times*, 2 April 1938
2. *Montgomeryshire Collections* 77, pp.60-62
3. *Montgomeryshire Express*, 1879
4. *The Montgomery County Times*, 18 November 1899
5. Bowling Green Society Minutes, 1778-1809, NLW
6. Two score sheets Cricket match Lymore, 1851, NLW
7. *Montgomeryshire Express*, 25 February 1879
8. *Montgomeryshire Express*, 20 June 1882

Chapter 15 Celebrations and Events
1. *An account of Rejoicings in the Counties of Montgomery and Salop in honor of the Coming-of age of The Viscount Lord Clive eldest son of the Right Hon. The Earl of Powis November 5th 1839*, printed by R. Owen, Broad Street, Welshpool

Index

Illustrations in italic type